FUTURES TRADING 101

A STEP-BY-STEP GUIDE AND STRATEGIES FOR BEGINNER TRADERS

Usiere Uko

13: Market Sentiment and News Analysis 55

14: Interpreting Supply and Demand Factors 60

PART 5: BASIC FUTURES TRADING STRATEGIES 64

15: Long and Short Positions 65

16: Day Trading Futures 70

17: Swing Trading Strategies 75

18: Trend-Following Strategies 80

19: Range Trading Strategies 88

PART 6: RISK MANAGEMENT IN FUTURES TRADING 94

20: Setting Stop-Loss Orders 95

21: Managing Position Sizes and Leverage 100

22: Hedging Strategies with Futures 105

23: Diversification and Portfolio Allocation 109

PART 7: TRADING FUTURES ON VARIOUS INSTRUMENTS 113

24: Trading Stocks Futures 114

25: Trading Forex Futures 119

26: Trading Commodity Futures 125

27: Trading Crypto Futures 131

28: Trading Index Futures 137

29: Trading Interest Rate Futures 143

PART 8: ADVANCED TRADING TECHNIQUES 149

30: Spread Trading: Calendar Spreads and Intermarket Spreads 150

31: Options on Futures 155

32: Automated Trading and Algorithmic Strategies 159

PART 9: DEVELOPING A TRADING PLAN 164

33: Goal Setting and Risk Tolerance Assessment 165

34: Building a Trading Strategy 169

CONTENTS

Title Page

Copyright

Dedication

Introduction

PART 1: INTRODUCTION TO FUTURES TRADING   1

1: Understanding Futures Contracts   2

2: Advantages and Risks of Trading Futures   6

3: Key Participants in the Futures Market   10

PART 2: GETTING STARTED WITH FUTURES TRADING   13

4: Choosing a Futures Broker   14

5: Opening a Futures Trading Account   18

6: Margin and Leverage in Futures Trading   21

PART 3: FUNDAMENTAL CONCEPTS IN FUTURES TRADING   25

7: Contract Specifications and Terminology   26

8: Price Quotation and Tick Size   30

9: Understanding Margin Requirements   34

10: Calculating Profit and Loss in Futures Trading   39

PART 4: ANALYZING THE FUTURES MARKET   43

11: Fundamental Analysis for Futures Trading   44

12: Technical Analysis Tools and Indicators   49

...To new frontiers, learning and growing

35: Backtesting and Forward Testing   172

36: Psychology and Discipline in Futures Trading   176

PART 10: PRACTICAL CONSIDERATIONS   179

37: Market Access and Trading Platforms   180

38: Monitoring Trades and Performance Analysis   184

39: Tax Considerations for Futures Traders   187

40: Resources for Further Learning and Improvement   190

About The Author   195

Books In This Series   197

Books By This Author   199

INTRODUCTION

Welcome to *Futures Trading 101: A Step-by-Step Guide and Strategies for Beginner Traders*. If you are a beginner in futures trading, looking to start or curious about the exciting world of futures trading but don't know where to start, this book is for you. This book demystifies the process and provides you with the essential knowledge and strategies to begin your journey as a successful futures trader.

Trading futures can offer immense opportunities for financial growth, but it is essential to approach it with a solid understanding of its fundamental concepts, strategies, and risk management techniques. This comprehensive guide aims to equip you with the necessary foundation to navigate the futures market confidently.

In Part 1, we lay the groundwork by introducing you to the basics of futures trading. You will learn what futures contracts are, explore the advantages and risks associated with trading futures, and gain insights into the key participants in the futures market.

Part 2 guides you through the practical aspects of getting started with futures trading. From selecting a reliable futures broker to opening your trading account and understanding margin requirements, you'll have the tools to take your first steps into the market.

Building upon this foundation, Part 3 explores the fundamental concepts of futures trading, including contract specifications, price quotation, tick size, and calculating profit and loss. Understanding these essential elements is crucial for making informed trading decisions.

Analyzing the futures market is the focus of Part 4, where we delve into both fundamental and technical analysis techniques. You will discover how to evaluate supply and demand factors, interpret market sentiment, and use technical indicators to identify trading opportunities.

Part 5 introduces you to basic futures trading strategies. Whether you're interested in day trading, swing trading, trend-following, or range trading, this section provides a variety of approaches to suit your trading style.

Effective risk management is a critical aspect of successful futures trading, and Part 6 is dedicated to helping you understand and implement risk management techniques. You will learn how to set stop-loss orders, manage position sizes, employ hedging strategies, and achieve portfolio diversification.

In Part 7, we delve into advanced trading techniques, such as spread trading and options on futures. Additionally, we explore automated trading and algorithmic strategies that can enhance your trading efficiency and execution.

Developing a solid trading plan is the focus of Part 8. We guide you through goal setting, risk tolerance assessment, building a trading strategy, and the importance of psychology and discipline in futures trading.

Practical considerations for futures traders are covered in Part 9, including market access, trading platforms, performance monitoring, and tax considerations.

Throughout this book, we provide you with practical examples, tips, and insights to enhance your understanding and application of futures trading concepts. Additionally, we offer recommended resources for further learning and improvement.

Futures trading has its risks, and success requires dedication, knowledge, and continuous learning. By reading this book, you have taken an important step towards becoming a knowledgeable and confident futures trader.

So, let's embark on this exciting journey together as we dive into the world of futures trading and equip you with the skills and strategies to navigate the market with confidence and achieve your trading goals.

PART 1: INTRODUCTION TO FUTURES TRADING

1: UNDERSTANDING FUTURES CONTRACTS

In the world of financial markets, futures contracts play a vital role in facilitating the trading of various assets, from commodities like oil and gold to financial instruments like stock indices and currencies. Understanding the fundamentals of futures contracts is the first step towards becoming a successful futures trader. In this chapter, we will explore the key aspects of futures contracts and how they function.

WHAT ARE FUTURES CONTRACTS?

Futures contracts are legally binding agreements between two parties to buy or sell a specific asset at a predetermined price on a future date. These contracts are standardized in terms of quantity, quality, delivery date, and delivery location. Futures contracts are traded on organized exchanges, providing a transparent marketplace for buyers and sellers.

Manufacturing companies, refineries, and other businesses that rely on raw materials for production often utilize futures contracts as a practical solution to secure sources and prices of those materials for an extended period. By entering into futures contracts, these companies can effectively manage their supply chain and avoid unexpected disruptions or price fluctuations.

For example, imagine you are a manufacturer that requires a significant amount of a specific raw material throughout the year. Instead of constantly monitoring the market and being exposed to potential availability issues or price volatility, you can use a futures contract to lock in the agreed-upon quantity and price in advance.

By doing so, you gain the assurance that the raw material will be available when needed, and the price will remain stable throughout the agreed-upon period. This proactive approach allows you to plan your production processes, budget effectively, and minimize the risk of unexpected cost increases or supply shortages.

In essence, futures contracts provide manufacturers and other businesses with the ability to secure their raw material requirements in advance, ensuring a smooth and predictable supply chain. By mitigating the uncertainty surrounding availability and price fluctuations, these businesses can focus on their core operations and long-term planning, ultimately enhancing their overall efficiency and profitability.

KEY ELEMENTS OF FUTURES CONTRACTS

To comprehend futures contracts fully, it is essential to grasp the following key elements:

Underlying Asset: Each futures contract is based on an underlying asset, which can be a physical commodity (such as crude oil or wheat), a financial instrument (such as a stock index or a currency pair), or even an intangible asset (such as an interest rate or weather conditions).

Contract Specifications: Futures contracts have standardized specifications, including the contract size or quantity, quality parameters, minimum price fluctuations (tick size), and expiration months. These specifications vary depending on the exchange and the asset being traded.

Contract Expiration: Every futures contract has a specified expiration date, beyond which it ceases to exist. At expiration, the contract is settled either through physical delivery of the underlying asset (in the case of physically settled contracts) or through cash settlement (in the case of cash-settled contracts).

Long and Short Positions: In futures trading, participants take either a long or a short position. A long position represents a commitment to buy the underlying asset, while a short position represents a commitment to sell it. These positions can be held until expiration or offset by taking an opposite position in the same contract.

PURPOSE OF FUTURES CONTRACTS

Futures contracts serve multiple purposes for market participants:

Price Discovery: By bringing buyers and sellers together in an open and transparent marketplace, futures contracts help establish fair and transparent prices for the underlying assets. The continuous trading and price dissemination facilitate price discovery.

Hedging: Futures contracts enable market participants to manage and mitigate risks associated with price fluctuations. Hedgers, such as farmers or oil producers, use futures contracts to lock in prices in advance, protecting themselves from adverse price movements.

Speculation and Investment: Speculators aim to profit from price movements in the futures market without any direct interest in the underlying asset. They provide liquidity and contribute to market efficiency. Additionally, futures contracts serve as investment vehicles for portfolio diversification and gaining exposure to specific asset classes.

Margin Requirements and Leverage: Futures trading involves the use of margin, which refers to the initial deposit required to initiate a position. Margin requirements are typically a fraction of the total contract value, allowing traders to leverage their capital. However, leverage amplifies both potential profits and losses, making risk management crucial.

Risks and Considerations: While futures trading presents opportunities, it also carries inherent risks. Price volatility, leverage, and market uncertainties can result in substantial gains or losses. It is crucial for traders to understand these risks and develop appropriate risk management strategies.

By understanding the fundamental concepts and mechanics of futures contracts, you have laid a solid foundation for your futures trading journey. In the following chapters, we will delve deeper into various aspects of futures trading, including strategies, analysis techniques, and risk management.

2: ADVANTAGES AND RISKS OF TRADING FUTURES

In the previous chapter, we explored the fundamentals of futures contracts. Now, let's delve into the advantages and risks associated with trading futures. Understanding these factors will help you make informed decisions and navigate the futures market effectively.

ADVANTAGES OF TRADING FUTURES

Liquidity and Market Accessibility: The futures market is highly liquid, offering ample trading opportunities and tight bid-ask spreads. This liquidity ensures that you can enter or exit positions with ease, even in large contract sizes. Additionally, futures markets operate globally, providing access to a wide range of assets and opportunities.

Leverage and Capital Efficiency: Futures trading allows you to control a larger position with a smaller initial investment through margin requirements. This leverage can amplify potential profits. However, it is crucial to manage leverage carefully, as it also increases the risk of losses.

Price Transparency and Fairness: Futures exchanges provide transparent price information, ensuring fair and equal access to market data for all participants. This transparency allows traders to make informed decisions based on real-time price quotes and market depth.

Diverse Asset Classes: The futures market offers a broad range of asset classes, including commodities, stock indices, currencies, interest rates, and more. This diversity allows traders to explore different markets and diversify their portfolios effectively.

Hedging and Risk Management: Futures contracts serve as valuable tools for hedging against price fluctuations. By taking offsetting positions in the futures market, businesses and individuals can protect themselves from adverse price movements and manage their exposure to various risks.

RISKS OF TRADING FUTURES

Price Volatility: Price volatility is a significant risk in futures trading. Rapid and significant price movements can lead to substantial profits or losses. Traders must be prepared for price fluctuations and have appropriate risk management strategies in place.

Leverage and Margin Calls: While leverage can enhance potential profits, it also amplifies losses. Excessive leverage can quickly deplete your trading account if the market moves against your position. Additionally, margin calls may require you to deposit additional funds if your account balance falls below the required maintenance margin level.

Market Risk and Uncertainty: Futures markets are influenced by various factors, including economic indicators, geopolitical events, and supply and demand dynamics. Market risks and uncertainties, such as unexpected news or market disruptions, can lead to significant price fluctuations.

Counterparty Risk: In futures trading, you rely on the counterparty's ability to fulfill their obligations. While regulated exchanges mitigate this risk to a certain extent, it is crucial to choose reputable brokers and clearinghouses to minimize counterparty risk.

Operational and Execution Risks: Trading futures involves operational and execution risks. These include technological failures, connectivity issues, and trade execution delays. Traders must choose reliable trading platforms and stay vigilant to minimize these risks.

RISK MANAGEMENT IN FUTURES TRADING

To mitigate the risks associated with futures trading, it is crucial to implement effective risk management strategies:

Position Sizing and Diversification: Determining appropriate position sizes based on your risk tolerance and account size is essential. Diversifying your portfolio across different assets and markets can also help spread risk.

Stop-Loss Orders: Implementing stop-loss orders allows you to set predetermined exit points to limit potential losses. These orders automatically close your position if the market reaches a specified price level.

Risk-to-Reward Ratio: Consider the risk-to-reward ratio for each trade. Aim for trades where the potential reward outweighs the potential risk, ensuring that your potential profits are greater than your potential losses.

Risk Assessment and Contingency Planning: Regularly assess the risks associated with your trading activities and adjust your strategies accordingly. Develop contingency plans for unexpected market events or adverse outcomes to minimize potential losses.

Ongoing Education and Analysis: Continued learning and staying updated with market trends and analysis techniques are crucial for effective risk management. Enhance your trading skills and knowledge through educational resources, technical analysis tools, and staying informed about market news and events.

By understanding the advantages and risks of trading futures, you are better equipped to navigate the market. The key lies in managing risks effectively and capitalizing on the opportunities presented by this dynamic and diverse market.

In the next chapter, we'll explore the key participants in the futures market—from hedgers and speculators to institutional investors.

3: KEY PARTICIPANTS IN THE FUTURES MARKET

The futures market is a vibrant ecosystem driven by various participants who play unique roles in shaping its dynamics. Understanding these key participants is essential for gaining insight into market behavior and the forces that drive price movements. In this chapter, we will explore the major players in the futures market.

HEDGERS

Hedgers are participants in the futures market who aim to mitigate risks associated with price fluctuations in the underlying asset. Hedging allows businesses and individuals to lock in prices for future transactions, thereby protecting themselves from potential losses.

For example, farmers may hedge their crop prices, and oil producers may hedge their production costs. Hedgers take offsetting positions in futures contracts to balance their exposure and stabilize their financial positions.

SPECULATORS

Speculators are participants who enter the futures market with the primary goal of profiting from price movements. Unlike hedgers, speculators do not have an underlying interest in the physical asset. They take positions based on their market analysis and predictions, aiming to buy low and sell high or sell high and buy low. Speculators provide liquidity to the market, as their buying and selling activities contribute to market efficiency and price discovery.

COMMERCIALS

Commercials refer to companies or entities that have a direct interest in the underlying asset being traded in the futures market. These participants may include producers, manufacturers, or consumers of the physical asset. Commercials utilize futures contracts to manage their exposure to price volatility and ensure a more predictable cost structure for their business operations. They often take positions that align with their underlying business interests.

INSTITUTIONAL INVESTORS

Institutional investors, such as pension funds, mutual funds, and hedge funds, are major participants in the futures market. These entities trade futures contracts on behalf of their clients or their own portfolios. Institutional investors often employ sophisticated trading strategies, leverage their large capital base, and have the ability to move markets with their substantial trading volumes. Their participation adds liquidity and depth to the futures market.

RETAIL TRADERS

Retail traders, including individual traders (like you) and small-scale investors, are an important segment of the futures market. With advancements in technology and increased accessibility, retail traders now have the opportunity to participate actively in futures trading. They trade futures contracts for various reasons, such as capital growth, portfolio diversification, or as a speculative activity. Retail traders often focus on specific markets or asset classes that align with their trading preferences and goals.

MARKET MAKERS AND FLOOR TRADERS

Market makers and floor traders are professionals who facilitate trading on the exchange floor. Market makers provide liquidity by continuously quoting bid and ask prices for specific futures contracts. They buy at the bid price and sell at the ask price, profiting from the bid-ask spread. Floor traders, also known as locals, execute trades on behalf of themselves or their clients. They typically operate on the exchange floor and engage in short-term trading strategies to profit from price movements.

CLEARINGHOUSES AND EXCHANGES

Clearinghouses and exchanges are the backbone of the futures market infrastructure. Clearinghouses act as intermediaries between buyers and sellers, ensuring the financial integrity of the market. They facilitate the settlement of trades, manage margin requirements, and guarantee the performance of contracts. Exchanges provide the trading platform and establish the rules and regulations governing futures trading. They maintain orderly markets, enforce contract specifications, and disseminate market data.

Understanding the key participants in the futures market provides valuable insights into market dynamics, supply and demand factors, and the interplay of different interests.

By studying the actions and motivations of these participants, traders can gain a deeper understanding of market sentiment and make more informed trading decisions.

In the next section, we will guide you through the practical steps necessary to begin your journey. From selecting the right broker and opening your trading account to understanding margin requirements, this section provides all the essential tools and information you need to confidently enter the market.

PART 2: GETTING STARTED WITH FUTURES TRADING

4: CHOOSING A FUTURES BROKER

Selecting the right futures broker is a crucial step in your journey as a futures trader. A reliable and suitable broker can provide you with the necessary tools, platform, and support to execute trades efficiently and effectively. In this chapter, we will explore the key factors to consider when choosing a futures broker.

REGULATORY COMPLIANCE AND REPUTATION

The first and foremost consideration when selecting a futures broker is their regulatory compliance and reputation. Ensure that the broker is registered with the appropriate regulatory bodies, such as the Commodity Futures Trading Commission (CFTC) in the United States or the Financial Conduct Authority (FCA) in the United Kingdom. Research the broker's track record, reviews, and client feedback to gauge their reputation and reliability.

It is essential to exercise caution and be wary of potential scams or fraudulent schemes. Unfortunately, the financial industry is not immune to individuals or organizations promising unrealistic returns or using deceptive tactics. If a futures broker promises exceptionally high returns or guarantees lucrative profits with minimal risk, it is a major red flag.

Trading futures inherently involves risk, and no legitimate broker can guarantee consistent or extraordinary returns. It is crucial to maintain a realistic outlook and understand that trading involves both winning and losing trades.

Beware of brokers who operate under a pyramid structure or utilize multilevel marketing arrangements. These schemes often rely on recruiting new participants to generate income, rather than focusing on genuine trading activities. Pyramid schemes are illegal and unsustainable, as they depend on continuously recruiting new members to sustain the structure.

A reputable futures broker should prioritize providing reliable trading services, transparent pricing, and access to markets, rather than relying on recruitment-based income models. Always research and investigate a broker's business model and ensure they operate in a legal and ethical manner.

TRADING PLATFORM AND TOOLS

Evaluate the trading platform provided by the broker. A user-friendly and technologically advanced platform can enhance your trading experience. Look for features such as real-time market data, charting tools, order types, and risk management features. Additionally, consider whether the platform is accessible across different devices and operating systems to suit your preferences.

ASSET COVERAGE AND MARKETS OFFERED

Consider the range of assets and markets offered by the broker. Ensure that they provide access to the futures contracts you are interested in trading. Look for a broker that covers a diverse range of asset classes, including commodities, stock indices, currencies, and interest rates. Having access to a wide variety of markets allows you to diversify your trading strategies and capitalize on different opportunities.

COMMISSION AND FEES

Compare the commission rates and fees charged by different

brokers. Consider both the per-trade commission and any additional fees, such as platform fees, data fees, or inactivity fees. While competitive pricing is important, also take into account the value provided by the broker in terms of platform features, customer support, and overall service quality.

CUSTOMER SUPPORT

Quality customer support is crucial, especially for new or less experienced traders. Ensure that the broker offers responsive and knowledgeable customer support through various channels, such as phone, email, or live chat. Prompt and reliable customer support can help address any issues or concerns that may arise during your trading journey.

ACCOUNT TYPES AND MINIMUM DEPOSIT

Consider the types of trading accounts offered by the broker and their suitability for your trading needs. Some brokers may offer different account types, such as individual accounts, joint accounts, or corporate accounts. Additionally, check the minimum deposit requirement for opening an account and ensure that it aligns with your budget and trading capital.

EDUCATIONAL RESOURCES AND RESEARCH TOOLS

Evaluate the educational resources and research tools provided by the broker. Look for educational materials, trading guides, webinars, and market analysis reports that can enhance your trading knowledge and skills. Access to comprehensive research tools, such as economic calendars, technical analysis tools, and news feeds, can also aid your trading decisions.

RISK MANAGEMENT FEATURES

Consider the risk management features offered by the broker. These may include features like stop-loss orders, limit orders, trailing stops, and guaranteed stop-loss orders. Effective risk management tools can help you protect your capital and manage your positions in volatile market conditions.

ACCOUNT SECURITY AND FUND PROTECTION

Ensure that the broker has robust security measures in place to protect your trading account and personal information. Look for brokers that offer secure login protocols, encryption, and segregated client funds. Check if the broker is a member of a compensation scheme or has insurance coverage to protect client funds in case of insolvency.

DEMO ACCOUNT AND TRIAL PERIOD

Consider whether the broker offers a demo account or a trial period. This allows you to test the broker's platform, features, and services without risking real money. It's an excellent way to assess the broker's suitability and compatibility with your trading style before committing funds.

By considering these factors and conducting thorough research, you can select a futures broker that meets your trading requirements and aligns with your goals.

The broker you choose will be your trading partner, so make sure they provide the necessary tools and support to enhance your trading experience.

In the next chapter, we'll walk you through the process of setting up your account, outlining the necessary documentation, account types, and other important factors to consider.

5: OPENING A FUTURES TRADING ACCOUNT

To participate in futures trading, you need to open a futures trading account with a reputable broker. Opening an account involves several steps and requires you to provide certain information. In this chapter, we will guide you through the process of opening a futures trading account.

RESEARCH AND CHOOSE A BROKER

Before opening an account, conduct thorough research and choose a broker that meets your trading needs and preferences. Consider factors such as regulatory compliance, reputation, trading platform, asset coverage, commission and fees, customer support, and educational resources. Selecting the right broker is essential for a smooth and successful trading experience.

COMPLETE THE APPLICATION FORM

Once you have chosen a broker, you will need to complete the account application form. This form collects information about your personal details, contact information, financial status, trading experience, and investment objectives. Provide accurate and truthful information to comply with regulatory requirements.

PROVIDE IDENTIFICATION AND VERIFICATION DOCUMENTS

To comply with Know Your Customer (KYC) and anti-money

laundering regulations, brokers will require you to provide identification and verification documents.

These documents typically include a government-issued identification document (e.g., passport or driver's license) and proof of address (e.g., utility bill or bank statement). Follow the broker's instructions regarding document submission.

FUND YOUR ACCOUNT

To start trading, you need to fund your futures trading account. Most brokers offer various funding options, such as bank transfers, credit/debit cards, or electronic payment systems. Follow the broker's instructions to deposit funds into your account.

Be aware of any minimum deposit requirements and consider the appropriate amount based on your trading capital and risk tolerance.

READ AND SIGN AGREEMENTS AND DISCLOSURES

Brokers typically provide agreements and disclosures outlining the terms and conditions of your futures trading account.

Read these documents carefully, as they specify important details such as trading rules, margin requirements, fees, and account maintenance procedures. If you have any questions or concerns, seek clarification from the broker before signing the documents.

SET UP TRADING PLATFORM AND ACCOUNT PREFERENCES

After your account is approved and funded, the broker will provide you with access to their trading platform. Download and install the platform according to the broker's instructions.

Once installed, customize the platform settings and preferences to suit your trading style. Familiarize yourself with the platform's features, order types, and risk management tools.

TEST AND PRACTICE WITH A DEMO ACCOUNT

Before trading with real money, take advantage of the broker's demo account if available. A demo account allows you to practice trading in a risk-free environment using virtual funds.

Utilize this opportunity to familiarize yourself with the platform, test trading strategies, and gain experience without risking your capital.

SECURE YOUR ACCOUNT

Maintaining the security of your futures trading account is crucial. Set up strong and unique passwords for your account and trading platform. Enable two-factor authentication if offered by the broker. Regularly monitor your account activity and promptly report any suspicious or unauthorized transactions to the broker's customer support.

CONTINUOUSLY EDUCATE YOURSELF

Even after opening a futures trading account, the learning process should continue. Engage in ongoing education and stay updated with market trends, news, and trading strategies. Utilize the educational resources provided by your broker and explore additional sources such as books, online courses, webinars, and forums. Continuous learning will enhance your trading skills and improve your chances of success.

By following these steps, you can open a futures trading account and begin your journey as a futures trader. Adhere to risk management principles, trade responsibly, and regularly assess and adjust your trading strategies as needed.

In the next chapter, we will break down how these tools allow you to control larger positions with a smaller amount of capital, potentially amplifying both gains and losses.

6: MARGIN AND LEVERAGE IN FUTURES TRADING

Margin and leverage are essential concepts in futures trading that have a significant impact on your trading capital and risk exposure. Understanding how margin works and how leverage can amplify your trading positions is crucial for effective risk management.

In this chapter, we will explore margin requirements, leverage ratios, and their implications in futures trading.

MARGIN REQUIREMENTS

Margin refers to the initial deposit you need to make to open and maintain a futures trading position. It serves as collateral or a performance bond that ensures you can fulfill your contractual obligations. The margin requirement is a percentage of the total contract value and is determined by the exchange or the broker.

INITIAL MARGIN

The initial margin is the minimum amount of funds you must deposit to open a futures position. It is calculated based on a percentage of the contract value and represents a fraction of the total value of the futures contract. The specific margin requirement varies depending on the exchange and the underlying asset being traded.

MAINTENANCE MARGIN

The maintenance margin is the minimum account balance that you must maintain to keep your futures position open. If the value of your account falls below the maintenance margin level, you will receive a margin call from your broker, requiring you to add funds to restore the account balance to the initial margin level. Failure to meet the margin call may result in the broker closing your position.

VARIATION MARGIN

The variation margin, also known as mark-to-market margin, represents the daily adjustment of your account balance based on the changes in the market price of the futures contract. At the end of each trading day, profits or losses on your open positions are added or subtracted from your account balance. Variation margin ensures that your account reflects the current market value of your positions.

LEVERAGE RATIO

Leverage allows you to control a larger position in the market with a smaller amount of capital. It magnifies both potential profits and losses. Leverage is expressed as a ratio, such as 10:1 or 50:1, indicating the multiple by which your position size is amplified compared to your trading capital. For example, with a 10:1 leverage ratio, a $1,000 trading capital allows you to control a $10,000 position.

PROS AND CONS OF LEVERAGE

The use of leverage in futures trading offers both advantages and risks. The main advantage is the ability to generate larger profits with a smaller capital investment. Leverage allows you to take advantage of price movements and market opportunities that would otherwise be inaccessible with limited funds. However, increased leverage also amplifies the potential for losses, as even small adverse price movements can result in significant drawdowns.

RISK MANAGEMENT WITH LEVERAGE

Managing risk is crucial when trading with leverage. Here are some key risk management considerations:

- Understand and assess the risk-reward profile of your trades before entering positions.

- Set stop-loss orders to limit potential losses and protect your trading capital.

- Avoid over-leveraging by using appropriate position sizing and risk per trade.

- Regularly monitor and review your positions to adjust or exit trades as needed.

- Continuously educate yourself on risk management techniques and strategies.

MARGIN CALLS AND LIQUIDATION

If the value of your account falls below the maintenance margin level, you will receive a margin call from your broker. A margin call requires you to deposit additional funds to meet the margin requirements.

Failure to meet the margin call may result in the broker liquidating your position to cover the losses. Liquidation ensures that the broker is protected and that your losses are limited to the amount of funds in your account.

SIMULATED TRADING AND DEMO ACCOUNTS

Before trading with real money and leverage, consider practicing with simulated trading or a demo account. These platforms allow you to trade using virtual funds and simulate real market conditions.

It's an excellent way to familiarize yourself with margin requirements, leverage effects, and risk management strategies without risking your capital.

SEEKING PROFESSIONAL ADVICE

If you are unsure about margin requirements, leverage, or risk management techniques, consider seeking professional advice from a financial advisor or experienced futures trader. They can provide guidance tailored to your specific trading goals and risk tolerance.

Understanding margin requirements and leverage is essential for effective risk management in futures trading. By being aware of the potential risks and rewards associated with leverage, and implementing proper risk management strategies, you can navigate the futures market with a disciplined approach.

In the next section, we'll explore the essential elements that drive the market, such as contract specifications, price quotations, tick sizes, and how to calculate profit and loss.

PART 3: FUNDAMENTAL CONCEPTS IN FUTURES TRADING

7: CONTRACT SPECIFICATIONS AND TERMINOLOGY

I n futures trading, understanding contract specifications and terminology is crucial for navigating the market and executing trades effectively. Each futures contract has specific attributes that determine its trading characteristics.

In this chapter, we will explore the key elements of contract specifications and commonly used terminology in futures trading.

UNDERLYING ASSET

Every futures contract is based on an underlying asset, which can include commodities (e.g., crude oil, gold), financial instruments (e.g., stock indices, currencies), interest rates, or other derivatives.

Understanding the nature and dynamics of the underlying asset is essential for analyzing market trends and making informed trading decisions.

CONTRACT SIZE

The contract size refers to the quantity of the underlying asset that each futures contract represents. It is typically standardized and defined by the exchange on which the contract is traded.

For example, a crude oil futures contract may represent 1,000 barrels of oil, while a stock index futures contract may represent a specific dollar value of the underlying index.

CONTRACT EXPIRATION

Futures contracts have a specified expiration date, after which they cease to exist. Traders need to be aware of the contract expiration and manage their positions accordingly. Prior to expiration, traders have the option to roll over their positions to the next contract month or close out their positions by offsetting them with opposite trades.

CONTRACT MONTHS AND DELIVERY MONTHS

Futures contracts are traded for different contract months, which represent specific time periods. For example, a futures contract may be available for trading in the months of March, June, September, and December. Within each contract month, there are also delivery months, which indicate the specific dates when physical delivery of the underlying asset can occur for certain contracts.

TICK SIZE AND TICK VALUE

The tick size refers to the minimum price increment at which a futures contract can move. It represents the smallest unit of price movement. Each tick has a corresponding tick value, which indicates the monetary value of a one-tick price change. Understanding the tick size and tick value is important for calculating potential profits or losses and managing risk.

MARGIN REQUIREMENTS

Margin requirements specify the initial and maintenance margin levels for trading futures contracts. These requirements ensure that traders have sufficient funds in their accounts to cover potential losses and fulfill their obligations.

Margin levels are set by the exchange or the broker and vary depending on the contract and market conditions.

ORDER TYPES

There are various order types used in futures trading to execute trades. Common order types include:

Market Order: An order to buy or sell a futures contract at the best available price in the market.

Limit Order: An order to buy or sell a futures contract at a specific price or better.

Stop Order: An order that becomes a market order when the market reaches a specific price, known as the stop price.

Stop-Limit Order: Similar to a stop order, but it becomes a limit order instead of a market order when the stop price is reached.

Market-if-Touched Order (MIT): An order to buy or sell a futures contract at a specified price or better, but only if the market touches that price.

Understanding the different order types allows you to execute trades with precision and control.

OPEN INTEREST

Open interest refers to the total number of outstanding futures contracts in a specific market. It represents the number of contracts that have been entered into but not yet closed out or delivered. Open interest provides insights into market liquidity and can help identify the level of trader participation in a particular contract.

SETTLEMENT METHODS

Futures contracts have different settlement methods, depending on the underlying asset and market specifications. The two common settlement methods are:

Cash Settlement: The contract is settled by exchanging cash payments based on the price difference between the entry price and the settlement price.

Physical Delivery: The contract is settled by physically delivering the underlying asset on the specified delivery date.

Understanding the settlement method is crucial, as it affects how profits or losses are realized.

By grasping contract specifications and familiarizing yourself with the relevant terminology, you will gain confidence in navigating the futures market and effectively communicating with other traders and market participants.

In the next chapter, we'll break down how to read price quotations and understand tick sizes, so you can make more precise and informed trading decisions.

8: PRICE QUOTATION AND TICK SIZE

Price quotation and tick size are fundamental aspects of futures trading that determine how price movements are measured and quantified. Understanding how prices are quoted and the significance of tick size is crucial for analyzing market movements and managing trading strategies.

In this chapter, we will explore price quotation methods, tick size, and their implications in futures trading.

PRICE QUOTATION METHODS

Futures contracts can be quoted using different price quotation methods, depending on the underlying asset and the exchange where the contract is traded. The two common methods are:

Decimal Pricing: In this method, prices are quoted in decimal format, such as $50.25 or $100.75. Decimal pricing provides a precise representation of price movements and is commonly used for financial instruments and some commodities.

Fractional Pricing: Fractional pricing uses fractions to quote prices, such as 1/8, 1/4, or 1/2. For example, a price quote of 100 1/4 represents a price of 100 and 1/4th of a point. Fractional pricing is often used in contracts related to agricultural commodities, such as grains and livestock.

Understanding the specific price quotation method used for a particular futures contract is important for interpreting price movements accurately.

TICK SIZE

Tick size refers to the minimum price increment at which a futures contract can move. It represents the smallest unit of price change and is predetermined by the exchange on which the contract is traded. Tick size varies across different futures contracts and is typically smaller for financial instruments compared to commodities.

For example, if the tick size of a crude oil futures contract is $0.01, it means that the contract can move in increments of one cent. In contrast, a stock index futures contract may have a tick size of 0.25 index points, indicating that price movements occur in quarter-point increments.

Understanding the tick size is essential for calculating potential profits or losses, determining stop-loss and take-profit levels, and managing risk.

TICK VALUE

Tick value represents the monetary value of a one-tick price change in a futures contract. It is calculated by multiplying the tick size by the contract's tick value multiplier. The tick value multiplier is determined by the exchange and is specific to each futures contract.

For example, if the tick size of a gold futures contract is $0.10 and the tick value multiplier is $10, the tick value would be $1 ($0.10 x $10). It means that every one-tick price movement in the gold futures contract represents a $1 change in value.

Understanding the tick value allows traders to quantify the potential profit or loss for each price movement and assess the risk-reward ratio of their trades.

IMPACT OF TICK SIZE ON TRADING STRATEGIES

Tick size plays a significant role in the development and execution of trading strategies. The tick size determines the minimum price movement required to generate a profit or trigger a stop-loss order. It influences the precision of entry and exit points and affects the frequency of trading activity.

Traders employing short-term, high-frequency trading strategies may focus on futures contracts with smaller tick sizes to take advantage of frequent price fluctuations. Conversely, traders using longer-term strategies may opt for contracts with larger tick sizes to avoid being overly sensitive to minor price movements.

ELECTRONIC TRADING AND DECIMALIZATION

With the advancement of technology, many futures exchanges have transitioned to electronic trading platforms and decimalization. Electronic trading allows for faster and more efficient order execution, while decimalization provides greater accuracy in price quotation and tick size.

The transition to decimalization has resulted in smaller tick sizes, allowing for more precise price movements and tighter bid-ask spreads. It has also facilitated the implementation of algorithmic trading strategies and increased market liquidity.

UNDERSTANDING PRICE QUOTATION AND TICK SIZE

To effectively analyze market movements and implement trading strategies, it is crucial to understand the specific price quotation method and tick size of the futures contracts you are trading.

Familiarize yourself with the conventions and tick value multipliers associated with different contracts to make informed trading decisions.

In the next chapter, we'll explore margin requirements in depth —how they work, why they matter, and how to manage them effectively.

9: UNDERSTANDING MARGIN REQUIREMENTS

Margin requirements play a vital role in futures trading as they determine the amount of funds you need to deposit to open and maintain positions. Understanding how margin requirements work is essential for managing risk, ensuring sufficient capitalization, and complying with exchange regulations.

In this chapter, we will explore the concept of margin, different types of margin requirements, and their implications in futures trading.

WHAT IS MARGIN?

Margin refers to the initial deposit or collateral that traders must provide to their brokers or exchanges to initiate futures positions. It serves as a form of security and ensures that traders can fulfill their financial obligations related to the contracts they hold.

By requiring margin, exchanges and brokers aim to mitigate counterparty risk and maintain the overall integrity of the futures market.

INITIAL MARGIN

Initial margin is the minimum amount of funds required to open a futures position. It represents a percentage of the total contract value and is set by the exchange or the broker. The specific initial margin requirement can vary based on factors such as the volatility of the underlying asset, market conditions, and regulatory requirements.

For example, if the initial margin requirement for a crude oil futures contract is 5%, and the total contract value is $100,000, you would need to deposit $5,000 as initial margin to open the position.

MAINTENANCE MARGIN

Maintenance margin refers to the minimum account balance that traders must maintain to keep their futures positions open. It is typically lower than the initial margin requirement but still ensures that traders have sufficient funds to cover potential losses.

If the account balance falls below the maintenance margin level, traders will receive a margin call from their brokers, requiring them to add funds to restore the account balance to the initial margin level.

Failure to meet a margin call may result in forced liquidation of positions by the broker to cover the losses, potentially incurring significant losses for the trader.

VARIATION MARGIN

Variation margin, also known as mark-to-market margin, represents the daily adjustment of the account balance based on the changes in the market price of the futures contract. At the end of each trading day, profits or losses on open positions are added or subtracted from the account balance.

If the position is in profit, the variation margin increases the account balance. Conversely, if the position is in a loss, the variation margin decreases the account balance. By adjusting the account balance daily, variation margin ensures that the account reflects the current market value of the positions.

SPAN MARGIN

Span margin is a specific method of calculating margin require-ments used by some exchanges. It employs sophisticated risk management models to estimate the potential risk and volatility of a futures position. The calculation takes into account factors such as historical price movements, market conditions, and cor-relation with other assets.

Span margin aims to provide a more accurate measure of the risk associated with a particular futures position, taking into con-sideration the specific characteristics of the contract and market conditions.

IMPACT OF MARGIN REQUIREMENTS

Understanding margin requirements is crucial for managing risk and capital efficiently. By having a clear understanding of the margin requirements, traders can:

- Determine the amount of funds needed to initiate and main-tain positions.
- Assess the risk-reward ratio of trades and adjust position sizes accordingly.
- Monitor account balances and manage margin calls effectively.
- Implement risk management strategies such as setting stop-loss orders to limit potential losses.

EXCHANGE AND BROKER VARIATIONS

It is important to note that margin requirements can vary between different exchanges and brokers. Each exchange and broker may have its own specific margin rules and requirements based on their risk management policies and regulatory obliga-tions.

It is essential to thoroughly review and understand the margin requirements set by the exchange and broker you are trading with, ensuring compliance and avoiding any unexpected margin calls or position liquidations.

MARGIN TRADING RISKS

While margin trading offers potential opportunities for increased returns, it also carries inherent risks. Some key risks to be aware of include:

Leverage Risk: Trading on margin amplifies both profits and losses. While leverage can enhance gains, it can also magnify losses, potentially resulting in substantial financial losses.

Margin Call Risk: If the account balance falls below the maintenance margin level, a margin call can be issued, requiring additional funds to be deposited. Failure to meet a margin call may lead to forced liquidation of positions.

Market Volatility Risk: High market volatility can lead to significant price swings, increasing the risk of margin calls and potential losses.

Overleveraging Risk: Excessive use of leverage can increase the risk of capital depletion and financial instability. It is crucial to use leverage prudently and manage risk effectively.

RISK MANAGEMENT STRATEGIES

To mitigate the risks associated with margin trading, it is essential to implement sound risk management strategies. Some key strategies include:

Proper Position Sizing: Determine the appropriate position size based on risk tolerance, account capital, and margin requirements. Avoid overexposing your account to excessive risk.

Stop-Loss Orders: Set stop-loss orders to limit potential losses. A stop-loss order automatically closes the position when the market reaches a specified price, helping to protect against adverse price movements.

Regular Account Monitoring: Regularly monitor your account balance, open positions, and margin requirements. Stay updated on market conditions and adjust positions or add funds as needed.

Education and Knowledge: Continuously educate yourself about risk management techniques, market analysis, and trading strategies. Stay informed about changes in margin requirements and exchange regulations.

By implementing effective risk management strategies and being aware of the potential risks involved in margin trading, you can safeguard your capital and navigate the futures market with greater confidence.

In the next chapter, we'll cover the critical process of calculating profit and loss in futures trading.

10: CALCULATING PROFIT AND LOSS IN FUTURES TRADING

Accurately calculating profit and loss is essential for evaluating the success of your futures trades and making informed trading decisions. By understanding the calculation methods and factors that affect profit and loss, you can assess the performance of your positions and adjust your trading strategies accordingly.

In this chapter, we will explore the process of calculating profit and loss in futures trading.

UNDERSTANDING POINT AND TICK VALUE

Before delving into profit and loss calculations, it's important to understand the concepts of point value and tick value. These values represent the monetary worth of price movements in a futures contract.

Point Value: Point value refers to the monetary value of one point or full price change in the contract. It varies depending on the specific futures contract and is determined by the exchange. For example, in a stock index futures contract, the point value may represent a certain dollar amount per index point.

Tick Value: Tick value represents the monetary value of one tick or minimum price movement in the contract. It is calculated by multiplying the tick size by the tick value multiplier. Tick value allows you to determine the profit or loss per tick movement in the contract.

Understanding the point value and tick value is crucial for accurately calculating profit and loss.

CALCULATING PROFIT AND LOSS

Profit and loss in futures trading are calculated based on the difference between the entry price and the exit price of a trade. The formula for calculating profit and loss is as follows:

Profit or Loss = (Exit Price - Entry Price) x Point Value / Tick Size

Let's break down this formula:

Exit Price: The price at which you close or exit your position.

Entry Price: The price at which you enter or open your position.

Point Value: The monetary value of one point or full price change in the contract.

Tick Size: The minimum price increment or tick size of the contract.

By substituting these values into the formula, you can determine the profit or loss for a specific trade.

Example Calculation

Let's illustrate the profit and loss calculation with an example:

Suppose you enter a long position in a crude oil futures contract at a price of $60.00 per barrel. You later exit the position at $62.50 per barrel.

The point value for this contract is $10 per point, and the tick size is $0.01 per barrel.

Profit or Loss = ($62.50 - $60.00) x $10 / $0.01 Profit or Loss = $2.50 x 1,000 Profit or Loss = $2,500

In this example, the profit from the trade would be $2,500.

FACTORS AFFECTING PROFIT AND LOSS

Several factors can affect the profit and loss calculation in futures trading:

Position Size: The size of your position, measured in contracts, affects the overall profit or loss. Larger position sizes amplify both gains and losses.

Commission and Fees: Transaction costs, such as commissions and exchange fees, should be considered when calculating profit and loss.

Slippage: Slippage occurs when the executed price differs from the expected price due to market volatility or order execution delays. Slippage can impact the realized profit or loss.

Margin Requirements: Margin requirements affect the capital tied up in a trade and can impact the potential return on investment.

PROFIT AND LOSS EVALUATION

Calculating profit and loss is not the sole measure of trading success. It's crucial to evaluate your profit or loss in relation to your risk and overall trading strategy. Key evaluation metrics include:

Risk-Reward Ratio: Assess the potential reward relative to the risk undertaken for each trade. A favorable risk-reward ratio indicates that the potential profit is higher than the potential loss.

Win-Loss Ratio: Evaluate the percentage of winning trades compared to losing trades. A higher win-loss ratio suggests more successful trades.

Return on Investment (ROI): Measure the overall return on investment based on the cumulative profit or loss from multiple trades.

By considering these evaluation metrics, you can gain a comprehensive understanding of your trading performance.

In the next section, we'll dive into the tools and techniques used to interpret market trends, including both fundamental and technical analysis.

PART 4: ANALYZING THE FUTURES MARKET

11: FUNDAMENTAL ANALYSIS FOR FUTURES TRADING

Fundamental analysis is a valuable approach to understand the factors that influence the supply and demand dynamics of the underlying assets in futures trading. By analyzing economic, geopolitical, and industry-specific data, fundamental analysis helps traders make informed trading decisions based on the intrinsic value of the assets.

In this chapter, we will explore the concept of fundamental analysis and its application in futures trading.

WHAT IS FUNDAMENTAL ANALYSIS?

Fundamental analysis involves evaluating the fundamental factors that drive the value of an asset. It focuses on understanding the underlying forces that affect supply and demand, such as economic indicators, company financials, geopolitical events, and industry trends.

The goal of fundamental analysis is to assess the fair value of an asset and identify potential market opportunities.

ECONOMIC INDICATORS

Economic indicators play a crucial role in fundamental analysis as they provide insights into the overall health of economies and specific sectors. Key economic indicators that impact futures trading include:

Gross Domestic Product (GDP): GDP measures the total value of goods and services produced within a country. It reflects the overall economic growth and can influence the demand for various assets.

Employment Data: Data such as non-farm payrolls, unemployment rates, and job creation numbers provide insights into the labor market. Employment data can impact consumer spending, corporate earnings, and sector performance.

Inflation Indicators: Inflation rates and consumer price indices (CPI) indicate the rate of price increases for goods and services. Inflation can impact interest rates, currency values, and the cost of raw materials, influencing the value of futures contracts.

Central Bank Policies: Monetary policies and interest rate decisions by central banks can significantly impact financial markets and currency values. Traders monitor central bank announcements to assess potential market movements.

GEOPOLITICAL EVENTS

Geopolitical events, such as political elections, government policies, trade disputes, and geopolitical tensions, can have a significant impact on futures markets. These events can disrupt supply chains, affect currency values, and influence investor sentiment.

Traders need to stay informed about geopolitical developments and their potential implications for the underlying assets in futures trading.

COMPANY AND INDUSTRY ANALYSIS

For futures contracts related to specific companies or industries, conducting company and industry analysis is essential. Factors to consider include:

Financial Statements: Analyzing company financial statements, such as balance sheets, income statements, and cash flow statements, can provide insights into a company's financial health and performance.

Industry Trends: Understanding industry-specific trends, such as technological advancements, regulatory changes, and consumer preferences, can help predict future demand and supply dynamics.

Company News and Events: Monitoring company news, earnings reports, product launches, and mergers and acquisitions can provide valuable information about the company's prospects and potential impact on futures prices.

COMMODITY AND SUPPLY-DEMAND ANALYSIS

For futures contracts related to commodities, analyzing supply and demand factors is crucial. Considerations include:

Supply Factors: Assessing factors such as production levels, weather conditions, geopolitical disruptions, and inventories can help gauge the potential supply of commodities.

Demand Factors: Evaluating factors such as economic growth, population trends, industrial activity, and consumer demand can provide insights into the demand dynamics for commodities.

Seasonal Patterns: Certain commodities exhibit seasonal price patterns due to factors like harvesting seasons, weather conditions, and holiday demand. Traders can utilize historical data to identify seasonal trends and incorporate them into their trading strategies.

USING FUNDAMENTAL ANALYSIS IN TRADING DECISIONS

Incorporating fundamental analysis into your trading decisions involves:

Gathering and Analyzing Data: Stay updated on relevant economic indicators, geopolitical events, company news, and industry developments. Analyze the data to identify trends, correlations, and potential market-moving factors.

Establishing Fair Value: Assess the fair value of the underlying assets based on fundamental factors. Compare current prices to their intrinsic value to identify potential overvalued or undervalued opportunities.

Trading Strategies: Develop trading strategies that incorporate fundamental analysis alongside technical analysis or other indicators. Consider both short-term and long-term perspectives when formulating your trading plan.

Risk Management: Utilize risk management techniques such as setting stop-loss orders and position sizing to protect against adverse market movements.

LIMITATIONS OF FUNDAMENTAL ANALYSIS

While fundamental analysis provides valuable insights, it has some limitations to consider:

Market Efficiency: Markets may already incorporate fundamental factors into prices, making it challenging to identify mispriced assets solely based on fundamental analysis.

Unexpected Events: Fundamental analysis may not anticipate sudden and unexpected events that can significantly impact market dynamics.

Interpretation Challenges: Interpreting fundamental data can be subjective, and different analysts may reach different conclusions. It's important to continuously refine your analytical skills and seek diverse perspectives.

INTEGRATING FUNDAMENTAL AND TECHNICAL ANALYSIS

Many traders combine fundamental analysis with technical analysis to gain a comprehensive view of the market. Technical analysis focuses on historical price patterns, trends, and chart patterns.

Integrating both approaches can provide a well-rounded perspective and enhance trading decisions.

In the next chapter, we'll dive into the world of technical analysis tools and indicators—from moving averages to oscillators and beyond.

12: TECHNICAL ANALYSIS TOOLS AND INDICATORS

Technical analysis is a widely used approach in futures trading that focuses on analyzing historical price patterns and market data to predict future price movements. Traders rely on various tools and indicators to identify trends, support and resistance levels, and potential trading opportunities.

In this chapter, we will explore some essential technical analysis tools and indicators used in futures trading.

CANDLESTICK CHARTS

Candlestick charts: moneysukh.com

Candlestick charts are a popular visual representation of price movements. They provide valuable information about the opening, closing, high, and low prices within a specific time period. Candlestick patterns can indicate potential trend reversals, market sentiment, and price volatility. Common candlestick patterns include doji, engulfing patterns, and hammer patterns.

MOVING AVERAGES

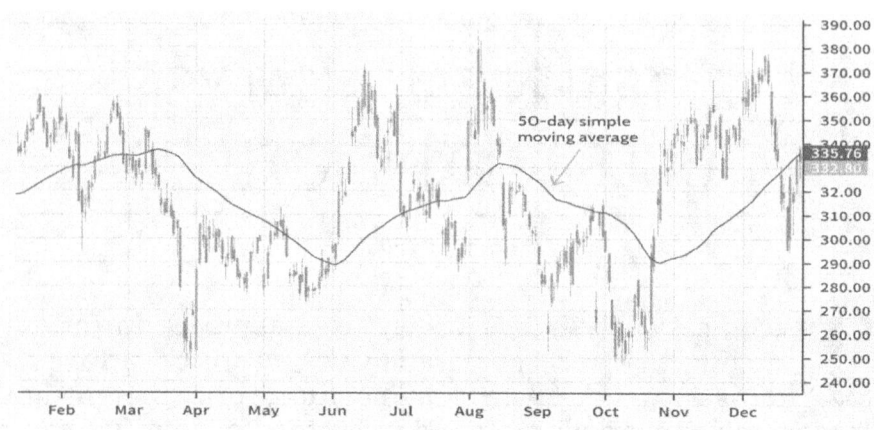

Simple Moving Average (SMA): investopedia.com

Moving averages are trend-following indicators that smooth out price data over a specific time period. They help traders identify the direction of the trend and potential support and resistance levels. Commonly used moving averages include the simple moving average (SMA) and the exponential moving average (EMA). Traders often use the crossover of different moving averages as a signal for trend reversals.

SUPPORT AND RESISTANCE LEVELS

Support and resistance: dailyfx.com

Support and resistance levels are price levels at which buying or selling pressure has historically caused the price to reverse or stall.

Traders use support levels as potential buying opportunities and resistance levels as potential selling opportunities. Support and resistance levels can be identified through trendlines, previous price highs and lows, or pivot points.

OSCILLATORS

Relative Strength Index (RSI) - bottom chart: commodity.com

Oscillators are technical indicators that help traders identify overbought or oversold conditions in the market. They provide insights into the potential exhaustion of a trend and possible trend reversals. Popular oscillators include the Relative Strength Index (RSI), the Stochastic Oscillator, and the Moving Average Convergence Divergence (MACD).

An RSI above 70 indicates overbought conditions, suggesting a potential price correction, while an RSI below 30 indicates oversold conditions, suggesting a potential price rise.

The MACD is calculated by subtracting the 26-period EMA from the 12-period EMA. A signal line (9-period EMA of the MACD) is then plotted on top of the MACD line, which can generate buy or sell signals when crossed. The MACD histogram, which plots the difference between the MACD line and the signal line, helps in identifying the strength of the trend.

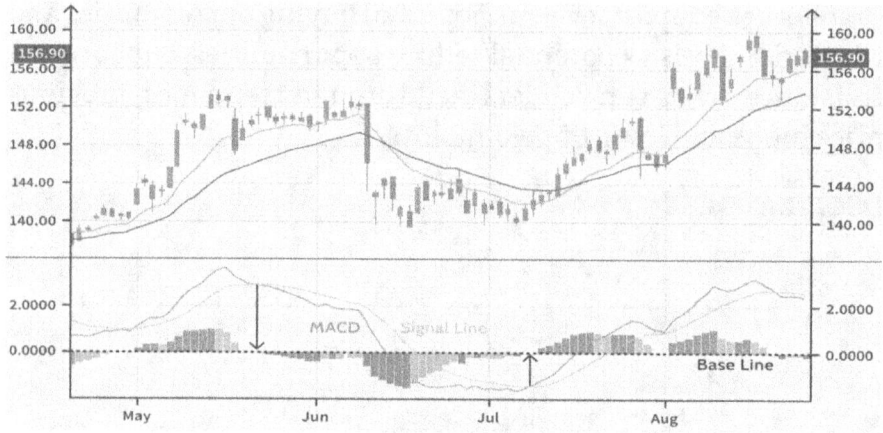

Moving Average Convergence Divergence (MACD): investopedia.com

Traders often look for divergences between the oscillator and price movements as a potential signal.

FIBONACCI RETRACEMENT

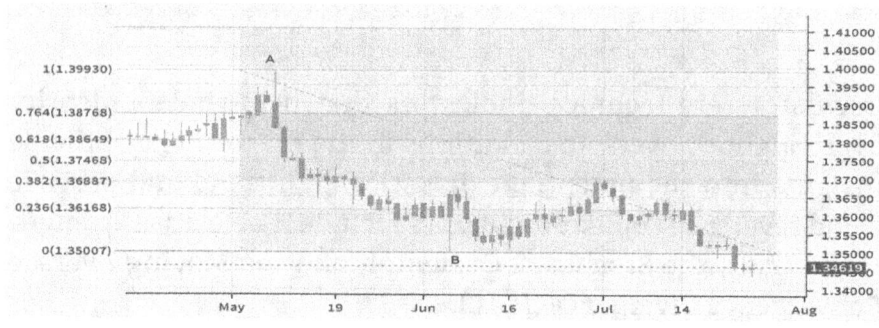

Fibonacci retracement: investopedia.com

Fibonacci retracement is a tool used to identify potential support and resistance levels based on the Fibonacci sequence. Traders draw Fibonacci retracement levels on a chart to determine areas where price corrections may occur.

The key levels are 23.6%, 38.2%, 50%, 61.8%, and 78.6%. Fibonacci retracement can help traders identify potential entry or exit points in a trend.

VOLUME ANALYSIS

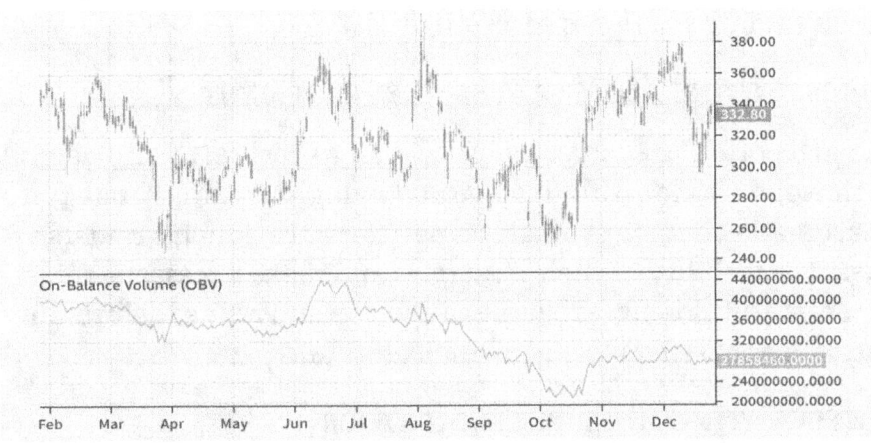

On-Balance Volume (OBV) indicator: investopedia.com

Volume analysis focuses on analyzing trading volume to understand the strength of price movements. High volume during price increases or decreases suggests strong market participation, confirming the validity of the trend. Traders often use volume indicators, such as volume bars or the on-balance volume (OBV) indicator, to assess market sentiment and confirm price movements.

CHART PATTERNS

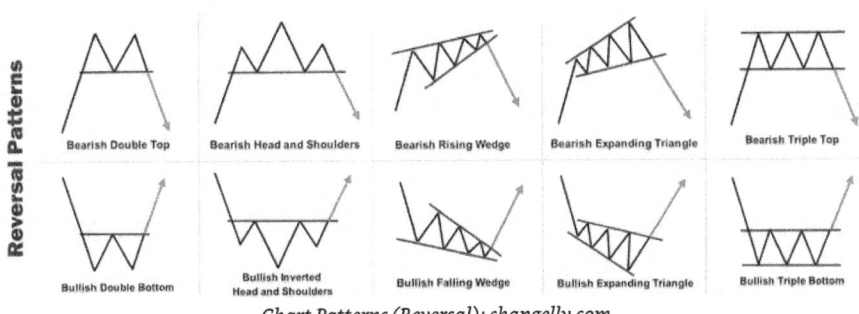

Chart Patterns (Reversal): changelly.com

Chart patterns are visual formations that occur on price charts and provide insights into potential future price movements.

Common chart patterns include triangles, double tops and bottoms, head and shoulders, and flags. Traders analyze these patterns to anticipate trend continuations or reversals and plan their trading strategies accordingly.

BACKTESTING AND STRATEGY DEVELOPMENT

Traders often use historical price data to backtest their trading strategies. Backtesting involves applying a trading strategy to past market data to evaluate its performance. It helps traders assess the viability of their strategies and make necessary adjustments. Additionally, traders can develop and refine their trading strategies based on technical indicators and patterns.

INTEGRATING MULTIPLE INDICATORS

Traders often combine multiple technical indicators to gain a comprehensive view of the market. By using different tools and indicators, traders aim to validate signals and increase the probability of successful trades.

However, it's important to avoid overcomplicating the analysis and to ensure that the selected indicators align with the trading strategy and time frame.

In the next chapter, we'll explore how investor emotions, market psychology, and breaking news can drive price movements.

13: MARKET SENTIMENT AND NEWS ANALYSIS

Market sentiment and news analysis play a vital role in futures trading as they provide insights into the overall market mood, investor sentiment, and potential impact on price movements. By understanding market sentiment and staying informed about relevant news events, traders can make more informed trading decisions.

In this chapter, we will explore the significance of market sentiment and news analysis in futures trading.

UNDERSTANDING MARKET SENTIMENT

Market sentiment refers to the overall attitude or mood of market participants toward a particular asset, market, or the overall economy. It can be bullish (positive) or bearish (negative) and can significantly impact price movements.

Market sentiment is driven by various factors, including economic indicators, geopolitical events, corporate earnings, and investor psychology.

IMPORTANCE OF MARKET SENTIMENT IN TRADING

Market sentiment provides traders with valuable insights into the prevailing market conditions and helps them gauge the potential direction of price movements. Key reasons why market sentiment is important in trading include:

Identifying Trend Strength: Market sentiment helps traders assess the strength of an existing trend. Strong bullish sentiment suggests a potential continuation of an uptrend, while strong bearish sentiment indicates a potential continuation of a downtrend.

Contrarian Trading Opportunities: Contrarian traders look for opportunities when market sentiment becomes excessively bullish or bearish. They aim to take positions opposite to the prevailing sentiment, anticipating a potential reversal in price movements.

Risk Management: Understanding market sentiment allows traders to assess the level of risk in the market. During periods of extreme optimism or pessimism, traders may choose to adjust their position sizes, tighten stop-loss orders, or adopt a more cautious approach to mitigate potential risks.

Market Timing: Market sentiment can provide clues about the timing of market entries or exits. Traders may choose to enter a trade when sentiment aligns with their analysis, increasing the likelihood of a favorable outcome.

NEWS ANALYSIS AND ITS IMPACT ON FUTURES TRADING

News analysis involves monitoring and analyzing relevant news events and their potential impact on the financial markets. News can be categorized into economic news (e.g., economic indicators, central bank decisions), geopolitical news (e.g., political events, trade disputes), and company-specific news (e.g., earnings reports, mergers and acquisitions).

Understanding the impact of news on futures trading is crucial for the following reasons:

Volatility and Price Movements: News events often lead to increased market volatility, which can result in significant price movements. Traders need to be aware of upcoming news releases and their potential impact on the futures market.

Market Reaction: News releases can trigger immediate market reactions. Positive news may lead to buying pressure, while negative news may result in selling pressure. Traders analyze news events and their potential impact on supply and demand dynamics to anticipate price movements.

Market Expectations: News releases are often compared to market expectations. If actual data or news deviates from expectations, it can lead to significant market reactions. Traders need to stay informed about consensus forecasts and market expectations to anticipate potential market moves.

Event-Driven Trading Opportunities: News events can create trading opportunities. Traders who react quickly to news releases may capitalize on short-term price movements driven by the news. However, it's important to exercise caution and consider risk management strategies when trading around news events.

RELIABLE NEWS SOURCES AND DATA FEEDS

Access to reliable news sources and timely data feeds is crucial for effective news analysis. Traders should consider using reputable news platforms, financial news websites, and data providers that offer real-time news updates, economic calendars, and relevant market analysis.

Additionally, traders can utilize social media platforms and specialized news feeds to stay updated on the latest market developments.

INCORPORATING MARKET SENTIMENT AND NEWS ANALYSIS IN TRADING

To incorporate market sentiment and news analysis in trading, traders can follow these steps:

Stay Informed: Keep track of relevant news events, economic indicators, and geopolitical developments that may impact the markets. Subscribe to reliable news sources, financial websites, and economic calendars to stay updated.

Analyze Market Reactions: Monitor how the market reacts to news events and assess the strength and duration of price movements. Look for patterns or correlations between news releases and market behavior.

Assess Market Sentiment: Gauge the prevailing market sentiment through indicators, surveys, or sentiment analysis tools. Consider sentiment indicators like the put/call ratio, volatility indexes, or sentiment surveys to get a sense of market participants' overall attitude.

Use News as Confirmation or Contrarian Signals: Incorporate news analysis alongside other technical or fundamental analysis tools to validate trading decisions. News can provide confirmation of existing trends or contrarian signals for potential reversals.

Risk Management: Consider the potential impact of news events on your trading positions and adjust risk management strategies accordingly. Set appropriate stop-loss orders, manage position sizes, and be prepared for increased market volatility during news releases.

Develop a News Trading Strategy: For traders interested in taking advantage of short-term price movements around news events, develop a news trading strategy. This may involve identifying high-impact news releases, setting predefined entry and exit points, and closely monitoring market reactions.

Maintain a Trading Journal: Keep a record of how news events and market sentiment influence your trades. Analyze the outcomes to identify patterns, strengths, and weaknesses in your trading approach and continuously improve your strategies.

News analysis and market sentiment should be used as one component of a comprehensive trading plan. It's important to integrate them with other technical and fundamental analysis techniques to make well-informed trading decisions.

In the next chapter, we'll explore how to interpret supply and demand factors across different asset classes and how they directly impact futures prices.

14: INTERPRETING SUPPLY AND DEMAND FACTORS

Interpreting supply and demand factors is a crucial aspect of futures trading. Supply and demand dynamics directly impact price movements in the futures market, and understanding these factors can help traders identify potential trading opportunities.

In this chapter, we will explore how to interpret supply and demand factors and their significance in futures trading.

SUPPLY AND DEMAND BASICS

Supply and demand represent the foundation of market economics. Supply refers to the quantity of a particular asset or commodity available in the market, while demand refers to the quantity that market participants are willing to buy at a given price.

The interaction between supply and demand determines the equilibrium price in the market.

KEY SUPPLY FACTORS

Supply factors can influence the price of futures contracts. Some important supply factors to consider include:

Production and Output: Changes in production levels or output can impact supply. Factors such as weather conditions, technological advancements, government policies, or geopolitical events can affect production capacities and, consequently, the supply of commodities.

Inventories and Storage Levels: Inventory levels of commodities can influence supply dynamics. Higher inventory levels may indicate excess supply, which can put downward pressure on prices. Conversely, low inventory levels may lead to supply shortages and potentially drive prices higher.

Seasonal Factors: Seasonal variations can impact supply. Certain commodities, such as agricultural products or natural resources, may have seasonal patterns that affect their availability. Traders need to consider these seasonal factors when analyzing supply dynamics.

KEY DEMAND FACTORS

Demand factors also play a significant role in determining futures prices. Some essential demand factors to consider include:

Economic Growth: Economic conditions and overall economic growth impact demand for various commodities. Strong economic growth often translates into increased demand for commodities used in industries such as construction, manufacturing, or transportation.

Consumer Demand: Consumer preferences and buying patterns influence demand for finished goods. Traders need to consider factors such as consumer spending habits, population demographics, and changes in lifestyle or consumer behavior when analyzing demand dynamics.

International Trade and Global Demand: Global trade and demand from international markets can significantly impact futures prices. Changes in international trade policies, geopolitical events, or shifts in global economic activity can influence demand for commodities.

INTERPRETING SUPPLY AND DEMAND IMBALANCES

Supply and demand imbalances occur when the quantity of a commodity demanded exceeds or falls short of the available supply. Understanding supply and demand imbalances is crucial for identifying potential trading opportunities. Here are some key aspects to consider:

Excess Supply: When supply exceeds demand, it can lead to downward pressure on prices. Traders may look for opportunities to sell or short futures contracts in anticipation of further price declines.

Supply Shortages: If demand outpaces supply, it can result in supply shortages and upward pressure on prices. Traders may consider buying or going long on futures contracts, anticipating further price increases.

Inventory Levels: Monitoring inventory levels can provide insights into supply and demand imbalances. Increasing inventories may suggest excess supply, while declining inventories may indicate tightening supply conditions.

IMPACT OF SUPPLY AND DEMAND ON PRICE PATTERNS

Changes in supply and demand dynamics can influence price patterns and trends in the futures market. Understanding these relationships can help traders identify potential entry and exit points. Here are a few scenarios to consider:

Trend Reversals: Shifts in supply and demand dynamics can lead to trend reversals. For example, a change from excess supply to supply shortages can trigger a bullish trend reversal, while a shift from supply shortages to excess supply can initiate a bearish trend reversal.

Breakouts and Breakdowns: Supply and demand imbalances

can contribute to breakouts or breakdowns from key support or resistance levels. Traders may look for these price patterns as potential signals for trend continuation or reversal.

Price Consolidation: Balanced supply and demand conditions may lead to price consolidation or sideways movements. Traders can use technical analysis tools, such as support and resistance levels or chart patterns, to identify potential breakout opportunities.

FUNDAMENTAL ANALYSIS AND SUPPLY-DEMAND RELATIONSHIPS

Fundamental analysis involves assessing the underlying factors that drive supply and demand dynamics. It encompasses evaluating economic indicators, geopolitical events, weather patterns, and other factors that impact supply and demand.

Traders who incorporate fundamental analysis into their trading strategies can gain a deeper understanding of supply and demand relationships and make more informed trading decisions.

MARKET SENTIMENT AND SUPPLY-DEMAND FACTORS

Market sentiment and supply-demand factors are closely interconnected. Shifts in market sentiment can influence perceptions of supply and demand, thereby impacting futures prices. Traders should consider how market sentiment aligns with supply and demand fundamentals to gain a comprehensive view of market conditions.

In the next section, we will explore some of the most commonly used strategies for trading futures, from day trading to trend-following and range trading.

PART 5: BASIC FUTURES TRADING STRATEGIES

15: LONG AND SHORT POSITIONS

L ong and short positions are fundamental concepts in futures trading that allow traders to profit from both rising and falling markets. Understanding how long and short positions work is essential for implementing various trading strategies and managing risk.

In this chapter, we will delve into long and short positions and their significance in futures trading.

LONG POSITION

A long position in futures trading refers to buying a futures contract with the expectation that the price of the underlying asset will increase. When a trader takes a long position, they are effectively going "long" on the market. The goal is to sell the futures contract at a higher price in the future and realize a profit.

SHORT POSITION

A short position in futures trading involves selling a futures contract with the anticipation that the price of the underlying asset will decline. When a trader takes a short position, they are going "short" on the market. The objective is to buy back the futures contract at a lower price in the future and profit from the price difference.

PROFITING FROM LONG AND SHORT POSITIONS

The profit potential from long and short positions depends on the direction of price movements and the entry and exit points chosen by the trader. Here's how traders can profit from each position:

Long Position: Traders profit from a long position when the price of the underlying asset increases. They can sell the futures contract at a higher price than the purchase price, realizing a profit equal to the price difference.

Short Position: Traders profit from a short position when the price of the underlying asset decreases. They can buy back the futures contract at a lower price than the selling price, capturing a profit equivalent to the price difference.

RISKS AND CONSIDERATIONS

Both long and short positions come with inherent risks and considerations that traders should be aware of:

Long Position Risks: The risk in a long position arises if the price of the underlying asset decreases instead of increasing. In this case, the trader may experience losses if they sell the futures contract at a lower price than the purchase price.

Short Position Risks: The risk in a short position occurs if the price of the underlying asset rises instead of declining. In such a scenario, the trader may face losses when buying back the futures contract at a higher price than the selling price.

Margin Requirements: Traders need to consider margin requirements when taking long or short positions. Margin is the initial amount of capital required to enter a futures contract, and maintaining sufficient margin is crucial to sustain positions.

Risk Management: Implementing effective risk management strategies is essential when trading long or short positions. Traders should set appropriate stop-loss orders to limit potential losses and consider position sizing relative to their account balance.

TRADING STRATEGIES USING LONG AND SHORT POSITIONS

Traders can employ various strategies using long and short positions to capitalize on market opportunities. Here are a few common strategies:

Trend Following: Traders can take long positions in an uptrend and short positions in a downtrend to align with the prevailing market direction.

Breakout Trading: Traders can enter long positions when the price breaks out above a key resistance level and short positions when it breaks down below a crucial support level.

Pair Trading: Traders can take long and short positions simultaneously on related assets, aiming to profit from the price divergence or convergence between the two.

Spread Trading: Traders can utilize spread strategies, such as calendar spreads or inter commodity spreads, to take advantage of price differentials between related futures contracts.

MANAGING POSITIONS AND EXITING TRADES

Managing positions and knowing when to exit trades is crucial for successful futures trading. Traders should consider various factors, such as profit targets, stop-loss levels, time horizons, and market conditions, when deciding to close a position. Here are a few key points to consider:

Profit Targets: Set profit targets based on technical analysis, fundamental analysis, or predefined risk-reward ratios. When the market reaches the desired profit level, consider closing the position to lock in gains.

Stop-Loss Orders: Implement stop-loss orders to limit potential losses. Set stop-loss levels based on risk tolerance, support and resistance levels, or volatility indicators. If the market moves against the position, the stop-loss order will trigger an automatic exit to prevent further losses.

Trailing Stops: Consider using trailing stops to protect profits as the market moves in favor of the position. Trailing stops automatically adjust the stop-loss level as the price moves in the desired direction, allowing traders to capture more significant gains while protecting against sudden reversals.

Time Horizons: Determine the desired time horizon for the trade. Some traders prefer short-term trades, while others take longer-term positions. Align the exit strategy with the intended time frame and adjust it if market conditions change.

Market Conditions: Monitor market conditions and adjust exit strategies accordingly. If there are significant changes in supply and demand factors, economic indicators, or unexpected news events, reevaluate the position and consider exiting if necessary.

LONG AND SHORT POSITIONS IN PORTFOLIO MANAGEMENT

Long and short positions can also be used in portfolio management to diversify risk and potentially enhance returns. By taking both long and short positions on different assets or sectors, traders can offset losses in one position with gains in another, thereby reducing overall portfolio risk.

Furthermore, long-short strategies can be employed in market-neutral trading approaches, where the focus is on capturing relative performance rather than directional market movements. This approach aims to identify assets that are expected to outperform or underperform their respective benchmarks, regardless of overall market direction.

LONG AND SHORT POSITIONS: A BALANCING ACT

Understanding long and short positions is essential for navigating the futures market successfully. Both positions offer unique opportunities and risks.

Traders must carefully analyze market conditions, employ effective risk management strategies, and adapt their approaches as market dynamics evolve.

In the next chapter, we'll explore how to take advantage of short-term price movements within a single trading day.

16: DAY TRADING FUTURES

Day trading futures is a popular and dynamic trading approach that involves opening and closing positions within the same trading day. Day traders aim to take advantage of short-term price movements, utilizing technical analysis tools, market indicators, and quick decision-making to generate profits.

In this chapter, we will explore the world of day trading futures, including strategies, techniques, and considerations for successful day trading.

UNDERSTANDING DAY TRADING FUTURES

Day trading futures differs from longer-term trading approaches as positions are typically opened and closed within the same trading session. This approach allows traders to capitalize on intraday price fluctuations without holding positions overnight, thereby avoiding potential overnight risks.

KEY ELEMENTS OF DAY TRADING FUTURES

To effectively engage in day trading futures, it is essential to understand and apply the following key elements:

Technical Analysis: Utilize technical analysis tools, including chart patterns, indicators, and trend analysis, to identify potential entry and exit points. Day traders heavily rely on technical analysis to make quick and informed trading decisions.

Volatility: Take advantage of the intraday volatility in futures markets. Volatility provides opportunities for profit as prices fluctuate, allowing day traders to enter and exit positions at advantageous price levels.

Liquidity: Focus on trading futures contracts that exhibit high liquidity. Liquid markets ensure that there are ample buyers and sellers, allowing for quick execution of trades without significant slippage.

Risk Management: Implement effective risk management techniques, such as setting stop-loss orders, managing position sizes, and adhering to predetermined risk-reward ratios. Risk management is crucial in day trading to protect capital and manage potential losses.

DAY TRADING STRATEGIES

Day traders employ various strategies to capitalize on short-term price movements. Here are some common day trading strategies used in futures markets:

Breakout Trading: Identify key support and resistance levels and enter positions when the price breaks out of these levels. Breakout traders aim to profit from strong price momentum and potential continuation of the trend.

Scalping: Engage in quick trades to capture small price movements. Scalpers aim to make multiple small profits throughout the trading day by taking advantage of minor price fluctuations.

Range Trading: Identify price ranges or channels and trade within those boundaries. Range traders aim to buy near support levels and sell near resistance levels, profiting from price oscillations within the range.

Momentum Trading: Identify strong trending moves and enter positions in the direction of the trend. Momentum traders aim to capture significant price moves driven by buying or selling pressure.

TOOLS AND INDICATORS FOR DAY TRADING

Day traders often utilize various tools and indicators to aid their decision-making process. Here are some commonly used tools and indicators for day trading futures:

Candlestick Charts: Analyze price patterns and identify key levels using candlestick charts. Candlestick patterns provide valuable insights into market sentiment and potential reversal or continuation patterns.

Moving Averages: Use moving averages to identify trends and potential entry or exit points. Moving averages smooth out price fluctuations and can serve as dynamic support or resistance levels.

Volume Analysis: Analyze trading volume to gauge market participation and the strength of price moves. High volume often accompanies significant price movements, indicating increased market activity.

Oscillators: Apply oscillators, such as the Relative Strength Index (RSI) or Stochastic Oscillator, to identify overbought or oversold conditions. These indicators can help traders anticipate potential reversals in price.

TRADING PLAN AND DISCIPLINE

Successful day trading requires a well-defined trading plan and discipline. Consider the following aspects when developing your day trading approach:

Pre-market Analysis: Conduct thorough pre-market analysis to identify potential trading opportunities, scan for news events, and assess market conditions before the trading session begins.

Trade Execution: Enter and exit trades with precision and discipline. Ensure that your entries and exits align with your trading plan and are based on sound analysis and risk management principles.

Journaling and Review: Maintain a trading journal to record your trades, strategies, and emotions. Regularly review your journal to identify strengths, weaknesses, and areas for improvement in your day trading approach.

Emotional Control: Emotions can play a significant role in day trading. Practice emotional control and discipline to avoid impulsive trading decisions driven by fear or greed.

Continuous Learning: The markets evolve, and so should your knowledge and skills. Commit to continuous learning and stay updated on market trends, new trading techniques, and risk management strategies.

DAY TRADING PITFALLS AND CONSIDERATIONS

While day trading futures offers potential profitability, there are risks and challenges to be aware of:

Market Volatility: Intraday price fluctuations can be significant, resulting in both profits and losses. High volatility requires careful risk management and the ability to make quick decisions.

Time Commitment: Day trading can be time-consuming, requiring constant monitoring of market movements and active trade management throughout the trading day.

Psychological Pressure: The fast-paced nature of day trading can create psychological pressure. It is crucial to manage stress, maintain discipline, and avoid emotional decision-making.

Trading Costs: Frequent trading can result in higher transaction costs, such as commissions and fees. Consider the impact of trading costs on profitability when engaging in day trading.

BUILDING A DAY TRADING ROUTINE

To optimize your day trading performance, develop a structured routine that aligns with your trading goals and preferences. Consider factors such as market opening times, research and analysis periods, trade execution, and self-improvement activities.

Day trading futures offers opportunities for traders to profit from short-term price movements within the same trading day.

By employing technical analysis, utilizing effective strategies, and maintaining discipline, day traders can navigate the challenges of intraday trading and potentially achieve consistent profitability.

In the next chapter, we'll discuss how to capture profits from market movements that occur over several days or weeks.

17: SWING TRADING STRATEGIES

Swing trading is a trading approach that aims to capture medium-term price swings in the futures market. Unlike day trading, swing traders hold positions for a longer duration, typically from a few days to several weeks, to capitalize on market trends and momentum.

In this chapter, we will delve into swing trading strategies, techniques, and considerations for successful swing trading in futures.

UNDERSTANDING SWING TRADING

Swing trading combines elements of both trend following and countertrend trading. It seeks to identify and capture price moves within established trends, allowing traders to profit from both upward and downward swings.

Swing traders focus on intermediate timeframes and aim to enter positions near key support or resistance levels when the market is likely to reverse or continue its trend.

KEY ELEMENTS OF SWING TRADING

To engage in swing trading successfully, it is essential to understand and apply the following key elements:

Trend Identification: Identify the overall trend in the market to align swing trades with the prevailing direction. Swing traders can use technical analysis tools, such as moving averages, trendlines, and price patterns, to identify and confirm trends.

Support and Resistance Levels: Identify significant support and resistance levels to determine potential entry and exit points. These levels act as barriers where price may reverse or experience temporary pauses, offering opportunities for swing trades.

Price Confirmation: Wait for price confirmation before entering swing trades. Price confirmation can come in the form of a breakout above resistance or a breakdown below support, accompanied by increased trading volume.

Risk Management: Implement effective risk management techniques, such as setting stop-loss orders, managing position sizes, and considering risk-reward ratios. Risk management is crucial in swing trading to protect capital and manage potential losses.

SWING TRADING STRATEGIES

Swing traders employ various strategies to identify and capitalize on market swings. Here are a few commonly used swing trading strategies:

Breakout Trading: Enter swing trades when the price breaks out of a consolidation phase or a significant resistance level. Breakout traders aim to profit from the continuation of a trend following the breakout.

Pullback Trading: Wait for price pullbacks or retracements within an established trend to enter swing trades at better prices. Pullback traders seek to join the overall trend at more favorable entry points.

Trend Reversal Trading: Identify potential trend reversals by looking for signs of exhaustion or divergence in price and indicators. Trend reversal traders aim to capture trend reversals and profit from the ensuing price movements.

Fibonacci Retracement Trading: Utilize Fibonacci retracement levels to identify potential support or resistance levels within a price correction. Swing traders may enter trades near these levels, anticipating a resumption of the prevailing trend.

TOOLS AND INDICATORS FOR SWING TRADING

Swing traders often employ various tools and indicators to aid their decision-making process. Here are some commonly used tools and indicators for swing trading:

Moving Averages: Use moving averages to identify trends, support, and resistance levels, as well as potential entry and exit points. Moving averages can help traders assess the overall market direction and capture swing trades within the trend.

Oscillators: Apply oscillators, such as the Relative Strength Index (RSI) or Stochastic Oscillator, to identify overbought or oversold conditions. These indicators can provide signals for potential trend reversals or market exhaustion.

Price Patterns: Identify chart patterns, such as double tops and bottoms, head and shoulders, or triangles, to anticipate potential price movements. Price patterns can indicate trend continuation or reversal opportunities for swing trades.

Volume Analysis: Analyze trading volume to confirm price moves and assess the strength of market trends. Increased volume during swing trades can provide validation and confidence in the potential profitability of the trade.

TRADE MANAGEMENT AND RISK CONTROL

Managing swing trades and controlling risk are critical aspects of swing trading. Consider the following factors for effective trade management:

Profit Targets: Set profit targets based on the swing's projected price move or predefined risk-reward ratios. Swing traders may choose to partially or fully exit positions as the price reaches these targets to lock in profits.

Trailing Stops: Implement trailing stops to protect profits and allow for potential further gains. Trailing stops automatically adjust the stop-loss level as the price moves favorably, ensuring that profits are preserved in case of a trend reversal.

Risk Management: Set appropriate stop-loss orders to limit potential losses. Determine the maximum acceptable loss per trade based on risk tolerance and position size. Adhere to disciplined risk management principles to protect capital.

Position Sizing: Determine the appropriate position size for each swing trade based on risk management rules and account size. Avoid overexposure to a single trade and diversify across multiple positions if desired.

Monitoring and Adjustments: Continuously monitor swing trades and adjust stop-loss levels or profit targets as necessary. Pay attention to changes in market conditions, news events, or technical signals that may warrant trade adjustments or early exits.

PSYCHOLOGY AND DISCIPLINE IN SWING TRADING

Swing trading requires discipline and emotional control. Consider the following psychological aspects:

Patience: Swing trading involves holding positions for longer durations compared to day trading. Exercise patience to allow trades to develop and avoid exiting prematurely due to impatience or fear.

Discipline: Stick to your trading plan and strategy. Avoid impulsive trading decisions driven by emotions or external market noise. Maintain discipline in adhering to risk management rules and trade execution guidelines.

Confidence and Flexibility: Develop confidence in your swing trading approach through practice and experience. However, remain flexible and open to adjusting strategies or exiting trades if the market conditions change significantly.

BUILDING A SWING TRADING ROUTINE

To optimize your swing trading performance, develop a structured routine that aligns with your trading goals and preferences. Consider factors such as market analysis, research time, trade execution, and periodic reviews of your trades and strategies.

Swing trading in futures markets offers traders the opportunity to capture medium-term price swings and profit from market trends.

By employing technical analysis tools, utilizing effective strategies, and practicing disciplined risk management, swing traders can navigate market swings and potentially achieve consistent profitability.

In the next chapter, we'll explore how to identify and ride long-term market trends, allowing you to capitalize on sustained price movements.

18: TREND-FOLLOWING STRATEGIES

rend-following is a popular trading strategy employed by traders across various financial markets, including futures. The essence of trend-following strategies is to identify and capitalize on established market trends, aiming to ride the momentum and profit from price movements in the direction of the prevailing trend.

In this chapter, we will explore trend-following strategies, techniques, and considerations for successful trend trading in the futures market.

UNDERSTANDING TREND-FOLLOWING

Trend-following strategies are based on the principle that markets tend to exhibit persistent trends over time. Traders employing this strategy aim to identify and participate in these trends, whether they are upward (bullish) or downward (bearish).

Trend-following strategies can be applied to various timeframes, from short-term trends lasting days to long-term trends spanning months or even years.

KEY ELEMENTS OF TREND-FOLLOWING STRATEGIES

To effectively engage in trend-following trading, it is essential to understand and apply the following key elements:

Trend Identification: Accurately identify the direction of the prevailing trend, whether it is an uptrend, downtrend, or a sideways consolidation phase. Trend identification can be achieved through technical analysis tools, such as moving averages, trendlines, and price patterns.

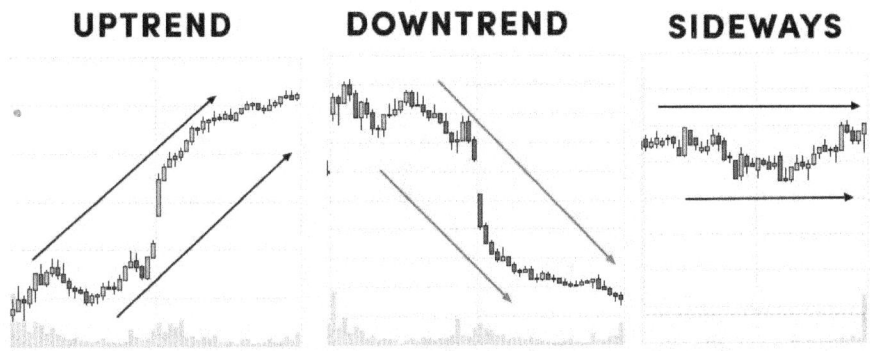

Trend Trading: danielsash.medium.com

Entry and Exit Points: Determine optimal entry points to enter a trade in the direction of the trend. This often involves entering a trade after a price breakout or retracement in the direction of the trend. Similarly, establish clear criteria or signals for exiting the trade, such as a trend reversal or the achievement of a predetermined profit target.

Risk Management: Implement effective risk management techniques to protect capital and manage potential losses. This includes setting appropriate stop-loss orders to limit downside risk, managing position sizes based on risk-reward ratios, and adhering to disciplined risk management principles.

TREND-FOLLOWING STRATEGIES

There are several trend-following strategies that traders can employ to capture and profit from market trends. Here are a few commonly used trend-following strategies:

Moving Average Crossover: This strategy involves using two or more moving averages of different time periods. When the shorter-term moving average crosses above the longer-term moving average, it generates a buy signal, indicating an up-ward trend. Conversely, when the shorter-term moving average crosses below the longer-term moving average, it generates a sell signal, indicating a downward trend.

Moving Average Crossovers: dailyfx.com

Trendline Breakout: Traders draw trendlines on price charts to identify the direction of the trend. When the price breaks above a downward trendline or below an upward trendline, it generates a signal to enter a trade in the direction of the breakout.

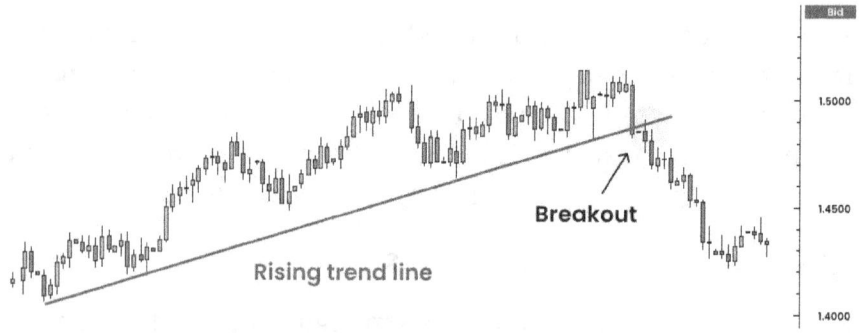

Trendline Breakout: blueberrymarkets.com

Price Patterns: Traders can utilize various price patterns, such as higher highs and higher lows in an uptrend or lower highs and lower lows in a downtrend, to identify and confirm the presence of a trend. Entry and exit points can be determined based on the formation and breakout of these patterns.

Parabolic SAR: The Parabolic Stop and Reverse (SAR) indicator is a trend-following indicator that provides potential entry and exit signals. It places dots above or below price candles to indicate potential trend reversals, signaling when to enter or exit trades.

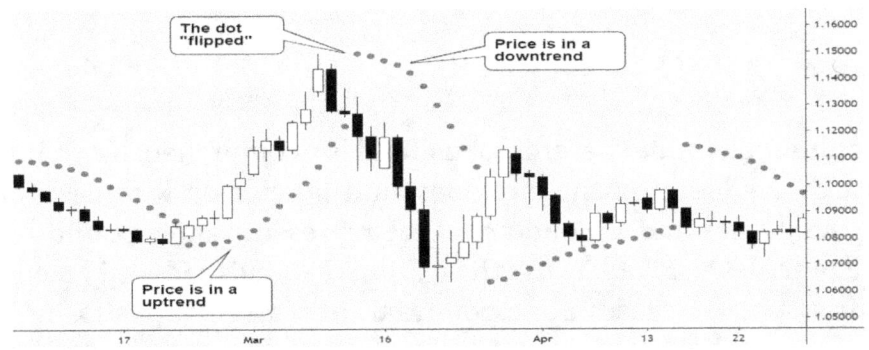

Parabolic Stop and Reverse (SAR): babypips.com

TOOLS AND INDICATORS FOR TREND-FOLLOWING

Traders often use specific tools and indicators to aid their trend-following strategies. Here are some commonly used tools and indicators for trend-following trading:

Moving Averages: Moving averages are versatile tools that help identify trends and potential entry and exit points. Traders use various types of moving averages, such as Simple Moving Averages (SMA) or Exponential Moving Averages (EMA), to smooth price data and capture trend signals.

Average Directional Index (ADX): The ADX is a popular indicator used to measure the strength of a trend. It helps traders determine whether a market is trending or consolidating. A rising ADX reading indicates a strengthening trend, while a declining ADX suggests a weakening trend or a sideways market.

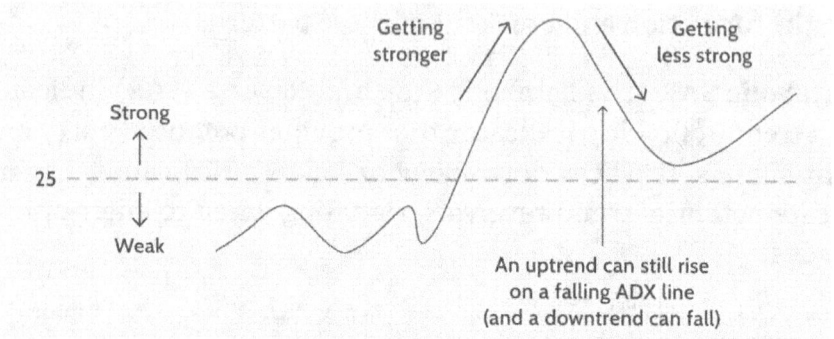

Average Directional Index (ADX): investopedia.com

Ichimoku Cloud: The Ichimoku Cloud is a comprehensive trend-following indicator that provides multiple signals. It consists of several lines and a cloud area that represents support and resistance levels. Traders use the Ichimoku Cloud to identify trend direction, momentum, and potential entry and exit points.

Ichimoku Cloud: investopedia.com

Relative Strength Index (RSI): The RSI is an oscillator that measures the speed and change of price movements. It helps identify overbought and oversold conditions, signaling potential trend reversals. Traders often combine RSI readings with other trend-confirming indicators to strengthen their trend-following strategies.

Bollinger Bands: Bollinger Bands consist of a moving average and two standard deviation bands. They help identify periods of high or low volatility and potential trend reversals. Traders look for price breaks or bounces off the bands as signals to enter or exit trades in the direction of the trend.

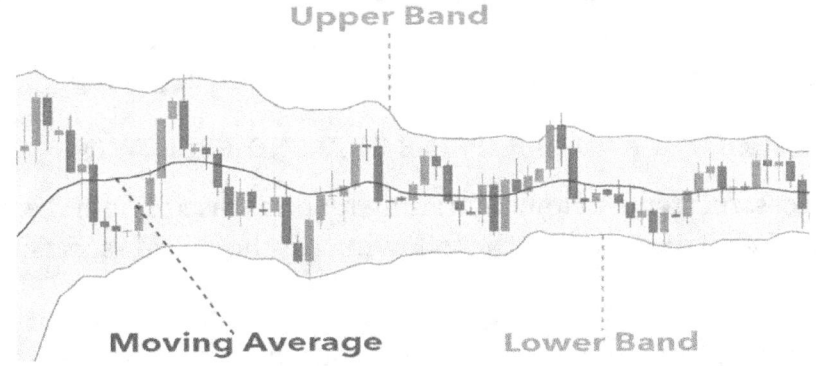

Bollinger Bands : dailyfx.com

TRADE MANAGEMENT AND RISK CONTROL

Effectively managing trades and controlling risk are crucial in trend-following strategies. Consider the following factors for trade management:

Trailing Stops: Use trailing stops to protect profits and capture potential further gains as the trend progresses. Trailing stops automatically adjust the stop-loss level as the price moves favorably, allowing traders to stay in the trade and maximize profits.

Pyramiding: Pyramiding involves adding to winning positions as the trend continues. Traders gradually increase their position size as the trade moves in their favor, enabling them to capitalize on extended trends. However, this technique should be used with caution, as it increases exposure and risk.

Exit Signals: Determine clear criteria for exiting a trade. This can include the violation of a trendline or moving average, a trend reversal pattern, or reaching a predefined profit target. Stick to the predetermined exit strategy to avoid premature exits or holding onto losing trades.

Review and Adaptation: Regularly review and evaluate your trend-following strategy to assess its effectiveness. Adapt and refine your approach based on market conditions, performance analysis, and feedback from trades. Continuous improvement is essential for long-term success in trend-following trading.

PSYCHOLOGY AND DISCIPLINE IN TREND-FOLLOWING

Successful trend-following trading requires discipline and emotional control. Consider the following psychological aspects:

Patience: Trend-following often requires patience, as trends can take time to develop and unfold. Avoid the temptation to enter trades based on short-term fluctuations or noise in the market. Stick to your strategy and wait for confirmation of a solid trend before entering trades.

Confidence: Develop confidence in your trend-following approach through practice and experience. Trust in the signals generated by your chosen indicators or strategies. However, remain open to adjusting or refining your approach as market conditions evolve.

Emotional Control: Emotions can interfere with objective decision-making. Manage emotions such as fear and greed by adhering to your trading plan, practicing disciplined risk management, and avoiding impulsive trades driven by emotional reactions.

BUILDING A TREND-FOLLOWING ROUTINE

To optimize your trend-following performance, develop a structured routine that aligns with your trading goals and preferences. Consider factors such as market analysis, trade execution, periodic reviews of your trades and strategies, and continuous learning.

Trend-following strategies offer traders the opportunity to capitalize on established market trends and profit from momentum.

By effectively identifying trends, determining entry and exit points, and employing appropriate risk management techniques, traders can potentially achieve consistent profitability in the futures market.

In the next chapter, we'll explore range trading strategies, which are designed to profit in markets that move within a defined price range.

19: RANGE TRADING STRATEGIES

R ange trading is a popular strategy employed by traders to capitalize on price movements within a defined range or boundary. Unlike trend-following strategies that aim to capture directional trends, range trading focuses on identifying support and resistance levels where price tends to oscillate.

In this chapter, we will explore range trading strategies, techniques, and considerations for successful range trading in the futures market.

UNDERSTANDING RANGE TRADING

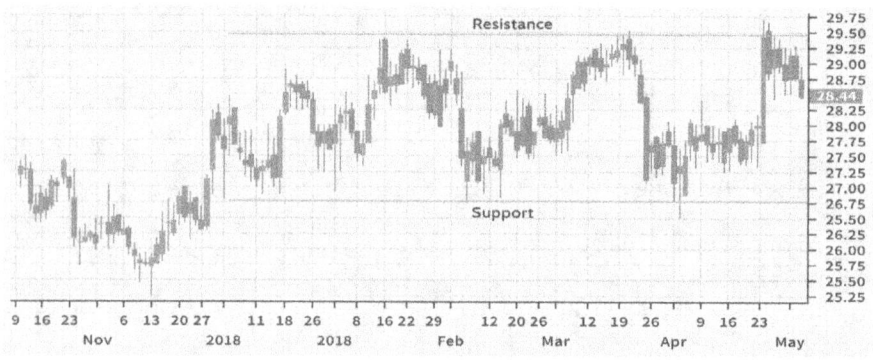

Range Trading: investopedia.com

Range trading involves identifying and trading price ranges where the market exhibits repetitive oscillations between established support and resistance levels. Traders aim to buy near support and sell near resistance, profiting from the price movements within the range. Range trading is suitable for markets that lack a clear trend or are consolidating.

KEY ELEMENTS OF RANGE TRADING STRATEGIES

To effectively engage in range trading, it is essential to understand and apply the following key elements:

Range Identification: Accurately identify the boundaries of the price range or the support and resistance levels where price tends to oscillate. This can be achieved through technical analysis tools such as horizontal support and resistance lines, channels, or Bollinger Bands.

Range Entry and Exit Points: Determine optimal entry points to buy near support or sell near resistance within the range. Traders often look for price reversals, candlestick patterns, or technical indicators signaling potential price exhaustion or reversals.

Establish clear criteria or signals for exiting the trade, such as reaching the opposite boundary of the range or achieving a predefined profit target.

Risk Management: Implement effective risk management techniques to protect capital and manage potential losses. This includes setting appropriate stop-loss orders outside the range boundaries, managing position sizes based on risk-reward ratios, and adhering to disciplined risk management principles.

RANGE TRADING STRATEGIES

There are several range trading strategies that traders can employ to capture and profit from price movements within a range. Here are a few commonly used range trading strategies:

Support and Resistance Bounces: This strategy involves buying near the support level and selling near the resistance level. Traders look for price bounces off these levels, entering long positions near support and short positions near resistance. They aim to profit from the repetitive price movements within the established range.

Breakout and Pullback: Traders employing this strategy wait for a breakout above the range resistance or below the range support. Once a breakout occurs, they enter a trade in the direction of the breakout, anticipating a continuation of the price move. They may also wait for a pullback to the breakout level to enter the trade, aiming to capitalize on a potential retest of the breakout.

Range Reversals: In range-bound markets, price often reverses near the range boundaries. Traders using this strategy look for signs of price exhaustion or reversal patterns near the range boundaries. They enter trades in the opposite direction of the recent price move, aiming to profit from price retracements or reversals within the range.

Range Volatility Breakouts: This strategy involves waiting for a significant increase in volatility within the range. Traders monitor volatility indicators or observe price patterns indicating a potential expansion in price range. Once volatility expands, they enter trades in the direction of the breakout, anticipating a larger price move beyond the previous range boundaries.

TOOLS AND INDICATORS FOR RANGE TRADING

Traders often use specific tools and indicators to aid their range trading strategies. Here are some commonly used tools and indicators for range trading:

Support and Resistance Levels: Identify key support and resistance levels using horizontal lines or trendlines. These levels act as barriers within the range, where price tends to reverse or consolidate.

Bollinger Bands: Bollinger Bands consist of a moving average and two standard deviation bands. They help identify periods of low or high volatility and potential range breakouts. Traders look for price breaks or bounces off the bands as signals to enter or exit trades within the range.

Oscillators: Oscillators such as the Relative Strength Index (RSI) or Stochastic Oscillator can indicate overbought and oversold conditions within a range. Traders look for divergences or extreme readings in these oscillators as potential signals for price reversals or range-bound conditions.

Range Expansion Indicators: Volatility indicators like Average True Range (ATR) or Bollinger Band Width can help identify periods of range expansion or contraction. Traders use these indicators to gauge the likelihood of a range breakout or expansion in price movement.

TRADE MANAGEMENT AND RISK CONTROL

Effective trade management and risk control are crucial in range trading strategies. Consider the following factors for trade management:

Stop-Loss Orders: Set appropriate stop-loss orders outside the range boundaries to limit potential losses in case of a range breakout or false breakout. Place stops beyond significant support or resistance levels to minimize the risk of being stopped out by minor price fluctuations within the range.

Profit Targets: Determine clear profit targets based on the range width or price oscillations within the range. Take profits near the opposite boundary of the range or based on technical indicators signaling potential exhaustion or reversal.

Monitoring Range Breakouts: Continuously monitor the range for signs of a breakout. If a breakout occurs, consider adjusting your strategy or exiting the trade to avoid being caught on the wrong side of a significant price move.

Risk-Reward Ratios: Maintain a favorable risk-reward ratio by ensuring that potential profits outweigh potential losses. Analyze each trade opportunity based on its risk-reward profile and only take trades that offer a sufficient reward potential compared to the risk taken.

PSYCHOLOGY AND DISCIPLINE IN RANGE TRADING

Successful range trading requires discipline and adherence to a well-defined trading plan. Consider the following psychological aspects:

Patience: Range trading often involves waiting for price to reach support or resistance levels before entering trades. Be patient and avoid the temptation to chase price or enter trades prematurely. Stick to your plan and wait for suitable entry opportunities within the range.

Adaptability: Markets can transition from trending to ranging conditions and vice versa. Be adaptable and adjust your strategy accordingly. Recognize when the market is transitioning and avoid using range trading strategies during trending phases.

Risk Control: Maintain discipline in risk management and avoid taking excessive risks or overtrading. Stick to your predetermined risk limits and avoid emotional decision-making driven by fear or greed.

BUILDING A RANGE TRADING ROUTINE

To optimize your range trading performance, develop a structured routine that aligns with your trading goals and preferences. Consider factors such as market analysis, trade execution, periodic reviews of your trades and strategies, and continuous learning.

Range trading offers traders the opportunity to profit from price movements within well-defined boundaries.

By effectively identifying ranges, determining entry and exit points, and employing appropriate risk management techniques, traders can potentially achieve consistent profitability in range-bound markets.

In the next section, we will delve into essential techniques to protect your capital and minimize potential losses.

PART 6: RISK MANAGEMENT IN FUTURES TRADING

20: SETTING STOP-LOSS ORDERS

In trading, managing risk is of utmost importance. One of the key risk management tools available to traders is the stop-loss order. A stop-loss order is a predefined order that automatically closes a trade if the market price reaches a specified level. It helps protect traders from excessive losses and allows for disciplined risk management.

In this chapter, we will explore the concept of stop-loss orders, their importance, and strategies for setting effective stop-loss levels in futures trading.

UNDERSTANDING STOP-LOSS ORDERS

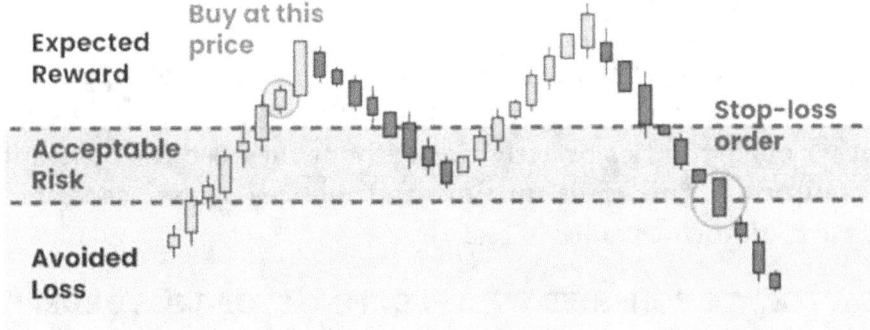

Stop-Loss Order: strike.money

A stop-loss order serves as a safeguard against adverse market movements. It is designed to limit potential losses by triggering the automatic closure of a trade at a predetermined price level. By setting a stop-loss order, traders define their maximum acceptable loss on a trade before entering it.

IMPORTANCE OF STOP-LOSS ORDERS

Stop-loss orders play a crucial role in risk management for several reasons:

Capital Preservation: A stop-loss order helps protect trading capital by preventing significant losses. It ensures that losses on individual trades are limited, reducing the impact of adverse price movements on overall account balance.

Emotional Discipline: Emotions can often cloud judgment and lead to impulsive decision-making. By setting a stop-loss order, traders remove the need to make subjective decisions in the heat of the moment. This promotes disciplined trading and prevents emotional reactions to market fluctuations.

Risk-Reward Ratio: Stop-loss orders allow traders to control their risk-reward ratios. By determining the distance between the entry point and the stop-loss level, traders can assess the potential loss compared to the potential profit on a trade. This helps maintain a favorable risk-reward ratio and aligns with a trader's risk tolerance.

Time Efficiency: Stop-loss orders provide a hands-off approach to managing trades. Once set, they allow traders to focus on other opportunities or activities without the need for constant monitoring. This frees up time and reduces stress associated with monitoring trades in real-time.

FACTORS TO CONSIDER WHEN SETTING STOP-LOSS ORDERS

When setting stop-loss orders, traders should consider the following factors:

Volatility: Consider the historical volatility of the market or instrument being traded. More volatile markets may require wider stop-loss levels to account for price fluctuations, while less volatile markets may allow for tighter stop-loss levels.

Support and Resistance Levels: Take into account significant support and resistance levels on the price chart. Placing stop-loss orders just beyond these levels can help avoid being stopped out by minor price fluctuations while still providing protection against significant price moves.

Timeframe: The trading timeframe can influence the placement of stop-loss orders. In shorter timeframes, stop-loss levels may need to be set closer to the entry point, whereas longer time-frames may require wider stop-loss levels to accommodate larger price swings.

Risk Tolerance: Every trader has a different risk tolerance. Set stop-loss levels that align with your risk tolerance and trading strategy. Conservative traders may opt for tighter stop-loss levels, while more aggressive traders may allow for wider stop-loss levels.

TYPES OF STOP-LOSS ORDERS

There are different types of stop-loss orders that traders can use, depending on their preferences and trading platforms. Some common types include:

Fixed Stop-Loss: A fixed stop-loss order is a static order that remains at a fixed price level. Once triggered, it immediately closes the trade. This type of stop-loss order is suitable for traders who prefer a straightforward approach to risk management.

Trailing Stop-Loss: A trailing stop-loss order adjusts the stop-loss level as the market price moves in the trader's favor. It trails the price at a specified distance, maintaining a dynamic stop-loss level. Trailing stops allow traders to lock in profits while still providing potential for further gains.

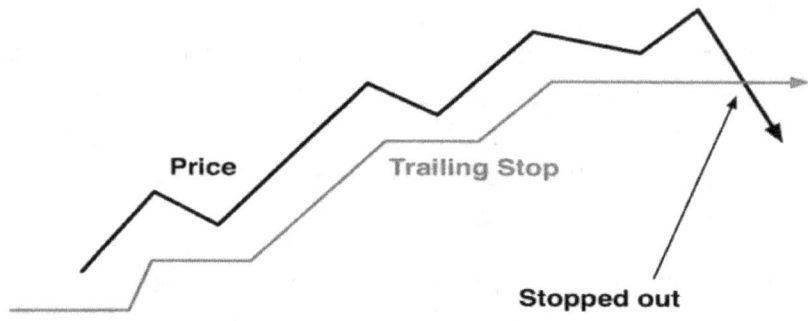

Trailing Stop-Loss: tradingtact.com

Time-Based Stop-Loss: Time-based stop-loss orders are set to automatically close a trade after a specific duration. They are useful for traders who prefer to exit trades if the expected price move does not materialize within a certain time frame.

ADJUSTING STOP-LOSS LEVELS

As market conditions change, it may be necessary to adjust stop-loss levels. Some situations that may warrant adjusting stop-loss orders include:

Price Consolidation: If the market enters a consolidation phase, adjust the stop-loss level to account for reduced price volatility. Traders may choose to tighten their stop-loss levels during periods of consolidation.

Profit Protection: As a trade moves in the trader's favor, adjusting the stop-loss level to lock in profits can be beneficial. This practice is often used in trailing stop-loss strategies.

News Events: High-impact news events can lead to increased market volatility. Consider widening the stop-loss level to provide the trade with enough breathing room to withstand potential price spikes or gaps resulting from the news.

Technical Factors: Significant technical developments such as trend reversals, breakouts, or pattern formations may necessitate adjusting the stop-loss level to reflect the new market conditions.

Setting effective stop-loss orders is an essential aspect of risk management in futures trading. By defining the maximum acceptable loss on a trade and implementing appropriate stop-loss levels, traders can protect their capital, maintain discipline, and manage risk effectively.

Understanding market volatility, support and resistance levels, risk tolerance, and adjusting stop-loss levels as needed are key considerations in optimizing stop-loss strategies.

In the next chapter, we'll explore how to determine the appropriate size of your trades and the impact of leverage on your overall risk exposure.

21: MANAGING POSITION SIZES AND LEVERAGE

Effective management of position sizes and leverage is crucial for traders to maintain proper risk management and achieve long-term success in futures trading. Position sizing determines the amount of capital allocated to each trade, while leverage amplifies the potential gains or losses.

In this chapter, we will explore the importance of managing position sizes and leverage, techniques for determining optimal position sizes, and strategies for responsible leverage usage in futures trading.

UNDERSTANDING POSITION SIZES

Position sizing refers to determining the appropriate quantity or value of contracts to trade based on the available trading capital and the desired risk exposure. Proper position sizing helps traders control risk, protect capital, and optimize the potential for returns.

IMPORTANCE OF POSITION SIZING

Effective position sizing is crucial for the following reasons:

Risk Management: Position sizing enables traders to limit their risk exposure on each trade. By allocating a specific percentage or amount of capital to each trade, traders can control the potential loss and prevent excessive drawdowns.

Capital Preservation: Proper position sizing ensures that traders do not risk a significant portion of their trading capital on a single trade. By diversifying their capital across multiple trades, traders reduce the impact of individual trade losses on their overall account balance.

Consistency: Implementing consistent position sizing rules promotes discipline and consistency in trading. It helps traders avoid impulsive decision-making and maintain a systematic approach to risk management.

Return Optimization: Optimal position sizing allows traders to maximize their potential returns while managing risk. By allocating the appropriate capital to trades with higher probabilities of success and adjusting position sizes based on market conditions, traders can seek to achieve consistent profitability.

TECHNIQUES FOR DETERMINING POSITION SIZES

There are several methods and techniques for determining position sizes. Here are a few commonly used approaches:

Fixed Percentage Risk: Traders allocate a fixed percentage of their trading capital, such as 1% or 2%, as the maximum risk per trade. The position size is then calculated based on the desired risk amount and the stop-loss level.

Fixed Dollar Risk: Traders determine the maximum dollar amount they are willing to risk on each trade. The position size is calculated by dividing the risk amount by the difference between the entry price and the stop-loss level.

Volatility-Based Position Sizing: Traders adjust their position sizes based on the volatility of the instrument being traded. For example, they may allocate smaller positions in more volatile markets and larger positions in less volatile markets to maintain consistent risk exposure.

Kelly Criterion: The Kelly Criterion is a mathematical formula that considers the probability of success and the risk-reward ratio to determine the optimal position size. It aims to maximize long-term growth while minimizing the risk of ruin.

UNDERSTANDING LEVERAGE

Leverage allows traders to control a larger position in the market with a smaller amount of capital. It magnifies both potential gains and losses. While leverage can amplify profits, it also increases the risk exposure. It is essential to understand leverage and use it responsibly to avoid excessive risk.

RESPONSIBLE USE OF LEVERAGE

To use leverage responsibly, traders should consider the following guidelines:

Risk Assessment: Before utilizing leverage, assess the risk associated with the trade and ensure that the potential reward justifies the increased risk exposure. Consider the market conditions, volatility, and potential impact of leverage on the trade.

Risk-Reward Ratio: Evaluate the risk-reward ratio of the trade and ensure it aligns with your trading strategy. Higher leverage may require a more favorable risk-reward ratio to compensate for the increased risk exposure.

Margin Requirements: Understand the margin requirements of the futures contracts being traded. Maintain sufficient account equity to meet margin obligations and avoid margin calls.

Risk Management: Implement appropriate risk management techniques, including setting stop-loss orders, diversifying trades, and monitoring positions closely. Adjust position sizes based on the leverage being used to ensure that risk exposure remains within acceptable limits.

MONITORING AND ADJUSTING POSITION SIZES AND LEVER-AGE

Traders should regularly monitor and review their position sizes and leverage usage to adapt to changing market conditions and account performance. Consider the following actions:

Periodic Evaluation: Assess the performance of your trades and trading strategy regularly. Analyze the impact of position sizes and leverage on your overall risk and returns. Adjust position sizes if necessary to maintain risk exposure within desired limits.

Adjusting Leverage: Evaluate the appropriateness of the leverage being used. Increase or decrease leverage based on market conditions, risk tolerance, and account equity. Exercise caution when considering higher leverage in volatile or uncertain markets.

Simulations and Backtesting: Use historical data and trading simulations to assess the impact of different position sizes and leverage levels on your trading strategy. This helps identify optimal settings and potential risks before applying them to live trading.

Proper management of position sizes and leverage is vital for effective risk management and long-term success in futures trading. By determining optimal position sizes, traders can control risk exposure, protect capital, and optimize returns.

Responsible usage of leverage ensures that traders carefully consider the associated risks and maintain risk management discipline.

Regular monitoring and adjustments of position sizes and leverage levels are essential to adapt to changing market conditions and account performance.

In the next chapter, Hedging Strategies with Futures, we'll explore how futures contracts can be used to safeguard your positions and offset potential losses.

22: HEDGING STRATEGIES WITH FUTURES

Hedging is a risk management technique used by traders and businesses to mitigate the potential impact of adverse price movements on their portfolios or operations. Futures contracts are widely used for hedging purposes due to their standardized nature and ability to provide price protection.

In this chapter, we will delve into the concept of hedging, explore various hedging strategies using futures, and discuss their application in different market scenarios.

UNDERSTANDING HEDGING

Hedging is the process of taking an offsetting position in the futures market to protect against price fluctuations in an underlying asset. It involves entering into a futures contract that moves inversely to the price movement of the asset being hedged. The goal of hedging is not to generate profits but to minimize potential losses or volatility.

TYPES OF HEDGING STRATEGIES

There are several common hedging strategies that traders employ using futures contracts. Let's explore a few of them:

Long Hedge: A long hedge involves buying futures contracts to protect against potential price increases in an underlying asset that a trader already owns. This strategy is commonly used by producers or businesses to secure a favorable price for their future production or inventory.

Short Hedge: A short hedge involves selling futures contracts to guard against potential price declines in an underlying asset that a trader plans to purchase in the future. This strategy is often used by consumers or businesses to lock in a favorable purchase price for their future needs.

Basis Hedging: Basis hedging aims to eliminate or reduce the price difference (basis) between the futures contract and the underlying asset. Traders take offsetting positions in the futures market to neutralize the basis risk and lock in a known relationship between the two prices.

Cross Hedging: Cross hedging involves hedging an asset using a futures contract that is not an exact match but has a high correlation to the asset being hedged. This strategy is employed when a direct futures contract for the asset is not available or when the correlation is strong between the asset and the futures contract.

APPLICATION OF HEDGING STRATEGIES

Hedging strategies using futures can be applied across various industries and market scenarios. Some examples include:

Commodity Hedging: Producers and consumers of commodities, such as agricultural products, energy resources, or metals, use futures contracts to hedge against price fluctuations. Producers can lock in selling prices, while consumers can secure purchase prices for their raw materials.

Equity Hedging: Investors can hedge their equity portfolios against market downturns by taking short positions in stock index futures. This helps offset potential losses and protects the value of their portfolios during market declines.

Currency Hedging: Businesses engaged in international trade can use currency futures contracts to hedge against currency exchange rate fluctuations. By locking in future exchange rates, they can reduce the risk associated with currency movements and ensure predictable cash flows.

Interest Rate Hedging: Financial institutions, such as banks or mortgage lenders, can hedge against interest rate fluctuations using interest rate futures contracts. This helps manage the risk associated with changes in borrowing or lending rates.

CONSIDERATIONS FOR HEDGING STRATEGIES

When implementing hedging strategies with futures, traders should consider the following:

Objective and Time Horizon: Clearly define the hedging objective and time horizon. Determine whether the goal is to protect against short-term price volatility or long-term price trends.

Correlation Analysis: Assess the correlation between the futures contract and the asset being hedged. A strong positive or negative correlation enhances the effectiveness of the hedging strategy.

Contract Selection: Choose the appropriate futures contract that closely aligns with the asset being hedged in terms of size, maturity, and contract specifications.

Monitoring and Adjustments: Regularly monitor the effectiveness of the hedge and make necessary adjustments based on market conditions. Reassess the hedge as the underlying asset or market dynamics change.

Hedging strategies using futures contracts provide traders and businesses with a powerful risk management tool. By taking offsetting positions in the futures market, hedgers can protect against adverse price movements and minimize potential losses. Long hedges, short hedges, basis hedging, and cross hedging are common strategies employed in various industries.

Understanding the application of hedging strategies, conducting correlation analysis, and selecting appropriate contracts are key considerations for successful hedging.

As we transition to the next chapter, Diversification and Portfolio Allocation, we will explore how to effectively spread risk across various instruments and asset classes.

23: DIVERSIFICATION AND PORTFOLIO ALLOCATION

Diversification and portfolio allocation are essential elements of successful trading and investment strategies. By spreading capital across different assets and markets, traders can reduce risk, enhance potential returns, and achieve a more balanced portfolio.

In this chapter, we will explore the importance of diversification, techniques for portfolio allocation, and considerations for constructing a diversified futures portfolio.

UNDERSTANDING DIVERSIFICATION

Diversification involves investing in a variety of assets that have low or negative correlation with each other. The goal is to create a portfolio that is not overly reliant on a single asset or market, thereby reducing the impact of any individual investment on the overall portfolio's performance. Diversification helps manage risk and potentially improve risk-adjusted returns.

BENEFITS OF DIVERSIFICATION

Diversification offers several key benefits:

Risk Reduction: By allocating capital across different assets or markets, investors can reduce the impact of any single investment on the overall portfolio. Diversification helps to mitigate the risk associated with specific assets or market segments.

Return Enhancement: Diversification can enhance potential returns by allowing investors to capture gains from various assets or markets that perform well over time. When one asset underperforms, other investments may compensate for the losses.

Volatility Reduction: A diversified portfolio tends to exhibit lower volatility compared to individual assets. This can provide a smoother investment experience and help investors navigate through market fluctuations.

Preservation of Capital: Diversification helps protect capital by minimizing the potential losses from any single investment. Even if a specific asset or market experiences a downturn, the impact on the overall portfolio is cushioned by the presence of other investments.

TECHNIQUES FOR PORTFOLIO ALLOCATION

When allocating capital to a diversified futures portfolio, consider the following techniques:

Asset Allocation: Determine the proportion of capital allocated to different asset classes, such as equities, fixed income, commodities, or currencies. The allocation should align with your investment objectives, risk tolerance, and market outlook.

Market Sector Allocation: Within each asset class, consider diversifying across different market sectors. For example, within commodities, allocate capital to agricultural, energy, or metals markets. This helps spread risk and capture potential opportunities in various sectors.

Geographical Allocation: Allocate capital across different geographical regions to diversify exposure to country-specific risks. Consider investing in futures contracts from various countries or regions to benefit from global market movements.

Time Horizon Allocation: Adjust the allocation based on your investment time horizon. Short-term traders may focus on liquid and highly volatile markets, while long-term investors may diversify across a broader range of assets and markets.

CONSIDERATIONS FOR DIVERSIFIED FUTURES PORTFOLIO

When constructing a diversified futures portfolio, consider the following:

Risk and Return Objectives: Define your risk tolerance and return objectives. Diversification should align with your risk appetite and desired returns. Higher-risk portfolios may allocate more capital to potentially higher-yielding but volatile assets.

Correlation Analysis: Assess the correlation between different futures contracts or market segments. Aim to include assets that have low or negative correlation with each other to achieve effective diversification.

Risk Management: Implement risk management techniques within each asset or market segment. Set appropriate stop-loss levels, monitor positions, and adjust allocations as needed to manage risk within the portfolio.

Portfolio Rebalancing: Regularly review and rebalance the portfolio to maintain the desired asset allocation. Adjustments may be necessary to align with changing market conditions, asset performance, or your investment objectives.

Diversification and portfolio allocation are vital components of a well-rounded trading and investment strategy. By diversifying across different assets, market sectors, geographical regions, and time horizons, traders can reduce risk and potentially enhance returns. Careful consideration of risk and return objectives, correlation analysis, and ongoing portfolio management are essential for constructing and maintaining a diversified futures portfolio.

In the next section, we will examine different types of futures contracts, including stocks, forex, commodities, cryptocurrencies, indices, and interest rates.

PART 7: TRADING FUTURES ON VARIOUS INSTRUMENTS

24: TRADING STOCKS FUTURES

Trading stock futures offers traders a unique way to speculate on individual stocks without needing to own the underlying shares. Stock futures are contracts that obligate the buyer or seller to purchase or sell shares of a particular stock at a predetermined price on a specified date in the future. They provide a leveraged and cost-effective way to gain exposure to the price movements of individual companies. In this chapter, we'll dive into the mechanics of trading stock futures, the opportunities they offer, and the risks involved.

WHAT ARE STOCK FUTURES?

Stock futures are derivative contracts based on the future price of a specific stock. These contracts are standardized agreements between two parties to buy or sell a particular stock at a predetermined price at a future date. Unlike options, which give you the right but not the obligation to exercise the contract, futures contracts must be fulfilled unless closed out before expiration.

Each stock futures contract represents a fixed number of shares, usually 100, making them an efficient way to speculate on stock movements. Stock futures allow traders to take both long and short positions, which can provide opportunities in both rising and falling markets.

HOW STOCK FUTURES WORK

When you trade stock futures, you're entering into a contract with another party to either buy (go long) or sell (go short) the stock at a later date. If the stock price moves in your favor, the value of your futures contract increases, allowing you to close the position for a profit. However, if the stock price moves against you, you'll incur a loss.

One of the major features of futures trading is leverage. When you trade stock futures, you don't need to pay the full value of the underlying stock upfront. Instead, you deposit a margin, which is a fraction of the total contract value. This leverage amplifies both potential gains and losses, so managing your risk is crucial.

WHY TRADE STOCK FUTURES?

There are several reasons traders are drawn to stock futures:

Leverage: Stock futures allow you to control a larger position with a smaller amount of capital, making it an efficient way to speculate on stock movements.

Hedging: Investors can use stock futures to hedge against adverse price movements in stocks they already own. For instance, if you hold shares of a stock but expect a short-term downturn, you can sell stock futures to offset potential losses.

Shorting Opportunities: Stock futures provide an easy way to short a stock, allowing you to profit from falling prices without needing to borrow the stock as you would in traditional short selling.

Liquidity: Many stock futures markets are highly liquid, which means traders can enter and exit positions quickly with tight bid-ask spreads.

EXAMPLE: TRADING STOCK FUTURES ON TESLA

Let's assume you believe Tesla's stock price will increase over the next three months. Tesla stock futures are trading at $500, and the contract represents 100 shares. You decide to go long one Tesla futures contract. Here's what might happen:

Scenario 1: Tesla's stock rises to $550 by the contract's expiration. You now have the option to sell the contract at $550, generating a $5,000 profit (100 shares × $50 increase).

Scenario 2: Tesla's stock drops to $450. You must sell the contract at $450, resulting in a $5,000 loss (100 shares × $50 decrease).

In both cases, the margin required for the position is a fraction of the total contract value, which increases your potential for profit (or loss).

RISKS OF TRADING STOCK FUTURES

While stock futures offer attractive opportunities, they also come with significant risks:

Leverage Risk: The use of leverage means that small price movements in the underlying stock can lead to substantial gains or losses. This makes it essential to manage your risk properly.

Expiration Risk: Stock futures have an expiration date. If the stock doesn't move in your favor by the expiration date, you'll have to close the position at a loss.

Volatility Risk: Individual stocks can be highly volatile, which means prices can fluctuate dramatically in a short period. While this creates opportunities, it also increases the potential for large losses.

KEY FACTORS INFLUENCING STOCK FUTURES

When trading stock futures, it's essential to consider the factors that influence stock prices:

Company Performance: Earnings reports, new product launches, and management decisions can have a direct impact on a company's stock price, influencing futures prices.

Economic Indicators: Broader economic conditions such as GDP growth, interest rates, and inflation can affect stock prices, particularly in sectors that are sensitive to economic shifts.

Industry News: News specific to an industry—such as regulatory changes, new competitors, or technological advancements—can impact stock futures related to companies within that industry.

Market Sentiment: General investor sentiment, whether bullish or bearish, can drive stock prices and stock futures, sometimes independent of fundamental factors.

HEDGING WITH STOCK FUTURES

One of the most practical uses of stock futures is for hedging. If you own a significant amount of a particular stock and you're concerned about short-term downside risk, you can sell stock futures to offset potential losses in the stock's price. For example, if you own 1,000 shares of a tech company but expect the market to decline in the near term, you could sell 10 futures contracts (each representing 100 shares) to protect your position.

DEVELOPING A STOCK FUTURES TRADING STRATEGY

When trading stock futures, it's essential to have a well-defined strategy. Here are some common approaches:

Trend Following: Identify long-term trends in a stock's price and trade futures in the direction of the trend.

Mean Reversion: This strategy involves trading futures when a stock's price moves away from its average value, expecting it to revert to the mean.

Breakout Trading: Enter positions when a stock's price breaks through key support or resistance levels, indicating a strong move in either direction.

Stock futures offer a powerful way to speculate on individual stocks or hedge existing positions with the use of leverage. However, they require a solid understanding of both the stock market and futures trading, as well as strict risk management practices.

With the potential for both significant profits and losses, careful planning and strategy development are essential.

As we move forward, let's explore the exciting world of Forex Futures in the next chapter, where we'll examine how to trade currency pairs using futures contracts and how global economic factors affect currency price movements.

25: TRADING FOREX FUTURES

F orex futures, also known as currency futures, offer a way to trade currency pairs using standardized contracts on an exchange. Unlike traditional forex (spot) trading, forex futures allow traders to speculate on the future value of one currency relative to another without the need for direct ownership of the underlying currencies.

In this chapter, we will explore the mechanics of trading forex futures, the advantages and risks involved, and how you can develop strategies to profit from movements in global currencies.

WHAT ARE FOREX FUTURES?

Forex futures are financial contracts that specify the price at which one currency will be exchanged for another at a predetermined date in the future. These contracts are standardized in terms of contract size, expiration dates, and margin requirements, making them highly accessible to traders on regulated exchanges.

A forex futures contract involves two currencies, often referred to as a currency pair (e.g., EUR/USD, GBP/JPY). The contract states how much of one currency will be exchanged for a specific amount of the other currency at a future date.

HOW FOREX FUTURES WORK

Each forex futures contract is tied to a specific currency pair, and it is traded in standardized units. For example, one contract of EUR/USD futures may represent 125,000 euros. When you buy a futures contract, you are essentially agreeing to buy euros and sell US dollars at a fixed price on a specified future date.

The price of the futures contract reflects the market's expectations for the relative value of the two currencies. If you believe that the euro will strengthen against the dollar, you would buy EUR/USD futures. Conversely, if you believe the euro will weaken against the dollar, you would sell the futures contract.

As with all futures contracts, forex futures are leveraged, meaning you only need to put down a margin (a fraction of the contract's total value) to control a larger position. This leverage can magnify both potential gains and losses.

WHY TRADE FOREX FUTURES?

There are several reasons why traders are drawn to forex futures:

Leverage: Forex futures allow traders to control large positions with a relatively small amount of capital, thanks to margin trading.

Transparency: Unlike spot forex trading, which takes place in decentralized markets, forex futures are traded on centralized exchanges, such as the Chicago Mercantile Exchange (CME), offering greater transparency.

Standardization: Forex futures are standardized contracts, meaning they have set expiration dates and contract sizes, making them easier to trade systematically.

Hedging: Companies that deal with international trade can use forex futures to hedge against currency risk, locking in exchange rates for future transactions.

KEY CURRENCY PAIRS IN FOREX FUTURES TRADING

When trading forex futures, you'll encounter a range of major currency pairs, each with different characteristics. Some of the most commonly traded forex futures pairs include:

EUR/USD: The euro versus the US dollar is the most traded currency pair in the world, making it a highly liquid and active market for futures traders.

GBP/USD: The British pound against the US dollar is another popular currency pair, often exhibiting higher volatility than EUR/USD.

USD/JPY: The US dollar versus the Japanese yen is a major pair influenced by interest rate differentials and global economic conditions.

AUD/USD: The Australian dollar versus the US dollar is a commodity-sensitive pair, influenced by the prices of commodities like gold and iron ore.

EXAMPLE: TRADING EUR/USD FUTURES

Let's assume you believe that the euro will strengthen against the US dollar over the next few months. The current price of EUR/USD futures is 1.1000, and you decide to buy one futures contract representing 125,000 euros. Here's how the trade might play out:

Scenario 1: The euro rises to 1.1200 by the expiration date of the contract. You decide to close your position, resulting in a profit. Each point move in the futures contract represents $12.50 (since the contract size is 125,000 euros), so your total profit would be $2,500 (200 points × $12.50).

Scenario 2: The euro declines to 1.0800. You close the position at a loss of $2,500 (200 points × $12.50).

In both cases, the leverage provided by futures magnifies your profits or losses compared to a spot forex trade of the same size.

ADVANTAGES OF TRADING FOREX FUTURES

Forex futures offer several key advantages:

Leverage: Futures contracts allow traders to control large positions with a relatively small initial margin, providing the potential for significant profits.

Standardization and Regulation: Forex futures are traded on centralized exchanges, ensuring transparency and reducing counterparty risk.

No Overnight Rollover Costs: Unlike spot forex, where positions are subject to rollover costs or credits when held overnight, futures contracts do not incur these charges.

Liquidity: Major currency pairs in forex futures tend to be highly liquid, meaning it's easier to enter and exit positions without significant slippage.

RISKS OF TRADING FOREX FUTURES

Despite their advantages, forex futures also come with risks:

Leverage Risk: The same leverage that offers profit potential can also lead to substantial losses, especially in volatile markets.

Interest Rate Differentials: Currency prices can be influenced by changes in interest rates in different countries, which can lead to sudden and unexpected price movements.

Geopolitical Risk: Currencies are often impacted by political events, such as elections, trade disputes, and geopolitical tensions, which can cause sharp moves in forex futures prices.

KEY FACTORS INFLUENCING FOREX FUTURES PRICES

Several factors can impact the price of forex futures:

Interest Rates: Differences in interest rates between the two currencies in a pair are one of the most important factors influencing currency prices.

Economic Indicators: Key reports such as GDP growth, employment data, and inflation figures can significantly impact the value of currencies.

Central Bank Policies: Decisions by central banks, such as raising or lowering interest rates, can lead to strong movements in forex futures.

Political Events: Elections, trade agreements, and international conflicts can all influence currency prices, sometimes causing significant volatility.

DEVELOPING A FOREX FUTURES TRADING STRATEGY

As with any type of futures trading, having a solid strategy is essential for success in forex futures. Here are a few popular approaches:

Trend Following: Identify and follow long-term trends in a currency pair. This strategy involves going long when the currency is in an uptrend and going short during downtrends.

Range Trading: Some currency pairs tend to trade within a defined range for extended periods. Traders can look for opportunities to buy at the bottom of the range and sell at the top.

Breakout Trading: Look for key technical levels such as support or resistance, and enter trades when the price breaks through these levels, signaling a potential large move.

Trading forex futures can be a profitable venture for those who understand the complexities of the currency markets and are prepared to manage the risks associated with leverage and volatility. By using futures to trade currencies, you can gain exposure to global economic trends and profit from both rising and falling markets.

In the next chapter, we'll move on to Trading Commodity Fu-

tures, where you'll learn how to speculate on the price movements of raw materials like oil, gold, and agricultural products
using futures contracts.

26: TRADING COMMODITY FUTURES

Commodity futures are one of the oldest and most well-established types of futures contracts, offering traders the opportunity to speculate on the prices of raw materials. From oil and gold to agricultural products like corn and wheat, commodity futures provide a means for investors to profit from fluctuations in the prices of physical goods. In this chapter, we'll explore the mechanics of trading commodity futures, key factors that influence commodity prices, and some effective strategies for success.

WHAT ARE COMMODITY FUTURES?

Commodity futures are standardized contracts that obligate the buyer to purchase, or the seller to deliver, a specified quantity of a physical commodity at a predetermined price and date in the future. Unlike spot markets where transactions occur immediately, commodity futures allow traders to speculate on the future price movements of commodities.

Commodity futures can be grouped into several broad categories, including:

- **Energy**: Oil, natural gas, gasoline, etc.
- **Metals**: Gold, silver, copper, platinum, etc.
- **Agricultural Products**: Corn, wheat, soybeans, coffee, sugar, etc.
- **Livestock**: Cattle, hogs, etc.

Traders often use these contracts to hedge against price fluctuations, but they are also a popular vehicle for speculation due to their high liquidity and volatility.

HOW COMMODITY FUTURES WORK

A typical commodity futures contract specifies the amount of the commodity, the price per unit, the expiration date, and the terms for delivery or settlement. For example, a crude oil futures contract might represent 1,000 barrels of oil, and the trader agrees to either buy or sell that quantity of oil at a fixed price on a future date.

However, most traders do not intend to take physical delivery of the commodity. Instead, they close their positions before the contract's expiration, locking in profits or cutting losses based on price movements.

Commodity futures are highly leveraged, meaning that traders can control large quantities of a commodity with a small upfront margin. While leverage offers the potential for significant gains, it also increases risk.

WHY TRADE COMMODITY FUTURES?

Commodity futures are attractive for several reasons:

Leverage: Similar to other futures contracts, commodity futures offer the ability to trade large positions with a fraction of the capital through margin requirements.

Hedging: Producers and consumers of commodities use futures contracts to hedge against price fluctuations. For example, a farmer may sell wheat futures to lock in a price for their harvest, while an airline might buy oil futures to secure fuel prices.

Liquidity: Many commodity futures markets are highly liquid, particularly for widely traded commodities like oil, gold, and corn. This allows traders to easily enter and exit positions.

Portfolio Diversification: Commodities often have low correlation with stocks and bonds, making them a valuable asset class for diversifying a portfolio.

KEY COMMODITIES IN FUTURES TRADING

There are many commodities traded on futures markets, but here are some of the most actively traded:

Crude Oil: One of the most widely traded and volatile commodities, crude oil futures (WTI and Brent) are influenced by global supply and demand, geopolitical factors, and OPEC decisions.

Gold: Often viewed as a safe-haven asset, gold futures are influenced by macroeconomic factors such as inflation, interest rates, and currency fluctuations.

Natural Gas: Natural gas futures are highly volatile and driven by weather conditions, storage levels, and energy demand.

Corn: As one of the most important agricultural products, corn futures are driven by factors such as crop yields, weather, and government policies.

Soybeans: Another crucial agricultural commodity, soybeans are used in food production and biofuel, with prices influenced by weather, demand, and trade policies.

EXAMPLE: TRADING CRUDE OIL FUTURES

Let's assume you believe that oil prices will rise in the coming months due to geopolitical tensions. You decide to buy a crude oil futures contract representing 1,000 barrels of oil at a price of $75 per barrel.

Scenario 1: Oil prices rise to $80 per barrel before the contract's expiration. You close your position for a profit. The price difference is $5 per barrel, so with 1,000 barrels, your profit would be $5,000.

Scenario 2: Oil prices drop to $70 per barrel. You close the position to avoid further losses. The price difference is $5 per barrel, resulting in a $5,000 loss.

ADVANTAGES OF TRADING COMMODITY FUTURES

Commodity futures offer several key benefits:

Volatility: Commodities are often more volatile than other assets, providing greater opportunities for traders to profit from short-term price movements.

Hedging: Futures contracts are used extensively by businesses to hedge against adverse price movements. For example, farmers may use futures to lock in a favorable price for their crops.

Global Economic Exposure: Many commodities are tied to global supply chains, making commodity futures a good way to trade macroeconomic trends.

Potential for High Returns: The leverage available in commodity futures can amplify returns, though it also increases the risk of losses.

RISKS OF TRADING COMMODITY FUTURES

While there are potential rewards, commodity futures also carry significant risks:

Leverage Risk: The high leverage involved in futures trading can lead to substantial losses if the market moves against you.

Supply and Demand Shocks: Commodities are highly sensitive to changes in supply and demand. Events like natural disasters, political unrest, or technological advancements can cause sharp and unpredictable price movements.

Seasonality: Many agricultural commodities are subject to seasonal fluctuations, which can create periods of heightened volatility and price unpredictability.

Market Manipulation: Some commodities, particularly oil and precious metals, are vulnerable to manipulation by large market participants, which can skew prices.

FACTORS INFLUENCING COMMODITY PRICES

The price of commodities is influenced by a variety of factors:

Supply and Demand: The most fundamental driver of commodity prices is the balance between supply and demand. Weather events, geopolitical tensions, and technological changes can all disrupt supply, while consumer demand fluctuates with economic conditions.

Macroeconomic Trends: Changes in inflation, interest rates, and economic growth can all impact commodity prices. For example, rising inflation may drive up gold prices as investors seek a store of value.

Geopolitical Events: Commodities like oil and natural gas are particularly sensitive to geopolitical tensions, such as conflicts in major oil-producing regions or trade wars.

Seasonal Patterns: Agricultural commodities are often affected by seasonal factors such as planting and harvesting cycles, weather conditions, and crop yields.

DEVELOPING A COMMODITY FUTURES TRADING STRATEGY

Here are a few popular strategies for trading commodity futures:

Trend Following: Identify and follow long-term trends in commodity prices. This strategy works well in markets with clear directional movements, such as during an oil price rally or a prolonged decline in gold prices.

Seasonal Trading: Some commodities, particularly agricultural products, exhibit predictable seasonal price patterns. Traders can take advantage of these patterns by entering and exiting trades based on the seasonality of the commodity.

Spread Trading: This strategy involves trading the price difference between two related commodities or between contracts with different expiration dates. For example, traders might simultaneously buy crude oil futures and sell gasoline futures to profit from the difference in price movements.

Commodity futures offer a unique opportunity to trade physical goods that are deeply tied to global economic conditions. With the right strategies and risk management practices, traders can profit from the volatility and price fluctuations in commodities ranging from oil and gold to agricultural products like corn and soybeans.

In the next chapter, we'll explore the exciting world of Trading Crypto Futures, where we'll delve into how futures contracts are used to speculate on the price of digital assets like Bitcoin and Ethereum.

27: TRADING CRYPTO FUTURES

C ryptocurrency futures have rapidly become one of the most exciting and volatile instruments in the futures market. With the rise of Bitcoin, Ethereum, and other digital assets, traders now have the opportunity to speculate on the future prices of these cryptocurrencies through futures contracts. In this chapter, we'll explore the mechanics of trading crypto futures, the unique factors that influence cryptocurrency prices, and strategies for successful trading in this fast-evolving market.

WHAT ARE CRYPTO FUTURES?

Crypto futures are contracts that allow traders to speculate on the future price of a cryptocurrency. These contracts function similarly to traditional futures contracts for commodities or stocks but are based on the price of digital assets like Bitcoin (BTC), Ethereum (ETH), and other cryptocurrencies.

When trading crypto futures, traders agree to buy or sell a specific amount of cryptocurrency at a predetermined price and date in the future. Crypto futures can be either cash-settled (no actual cryptocurrency is exchanged) or physically-settled (the cryptocurrency is transferred upon contract expiration).

Unlike spot trading, where you directly buy or sell cryptocurrencies at current market prices, crypto futures provide the opportunity to go long (buying to profit from price increases) or short (selling to profit from price decreases). This flexibility, combined with leverage, makes crypto futures an attractive option for traders looking to maximize their potential profits.

WHY TRADE CRYPTO FUTURES?

The popularity of crypto futures is driven by several key advantages:

Leverage: Crypto futures allow traders to control larger positions with a smaller amount of capital by using leverage. This can magnify profits, but also increases the risk of losses.

Hedging: Investors holding cryptocurrencies in their portfolio can use futures to hedge against price drops by taking short positions. For instance, if you own Bitcoin but fear its price may fall, you can short Bitcoin futures to protect your holdings.

Volatility: Cryptocurrencies are known for their extreme price volatility, which creates numerous opportunities for traders to profit from both upward and downward price swings.

24/7 Market: Crypto markets operate 24/7, unlike traditional financial markets. This constant trading allows crypto futures traders to take advantage of global price movements at any time.

Institutional Participation: Crypto futures have attracted significant interest from institutional investors, offering greater liquidity and enabling professional-level trading strategies.

HOW CRYPTO FUTURES WORK

Crypto futures operate similarly to other futures contracts, but with digital assets as the underlying instrument. Here's how they work:

Contract Specifications: Each crypto futures contract has specific details, including the size of the contract, the cryptocurrency being traded (e.g., BTC or ETH), the expiration date, and the tick size (the smallest price increment).

Leverage: Leverage allows traders to control a larger position with a smaller amount of capital. However, with crypto's inherent volatility, leverage can be a double-edged sword, amplifying both potential gains and losses.

Expiration and Settlement: Crypto futures typically have fixed expiration dates, after which the contracts are either cash-settled or physically settled. Some platforms, however, offer perpetual futures, which don't have expiration dates and are settled continuously.

Funding Rate: In perpetual futures, traders pay or receive a funding rate to keep their positions open. This rate ensures that the futures price stays in line with the spot price of the cryptocurrency.

POPULAR CRYPTOCURRENCIES IN FUTURES TRADING

While many cryptocurrencies are available for trading on futures markets, some of the most popular include:

Bitcoin (BTC): As the first and largest cryptocurrency by market cap, Bitcoin futures are the most widely traded crypto futures contracts. Bitcoin futures are offered by major exchanges like the Chicago Mercantile Exchange (CME), Binance, and BitMEX.

Ethereum (ETH): Ethereum, the second-largest cryptocurrency, is also widely traded in futures markets. Ethereum futures allow traders to speculate on the future price of the ETH token, which powers the Ethereum network.

Other Altcoins: In addition to BTC and ETH, some platforms offer futures on altcoins like Litecoin (LTC), Ripple (XRP), Solana (SOL), and others. However, these tend to be more volatile and less liquid than BTC and ETH futures.

FACTORS INFLUENCING CRYPTOCURRENCY PRICES

Several factors drive the prices of cryptocurrencies, making crypto futures a dynamic market. Key influences include:

Market Sentiment: Crypto prices are highly sensitive to market sentiment. News of regulatory changes, technological developments, or institutional adoption can significantly impact prices.

For example, when major companies like Tesla announced Bitcoin purchases, the price surged.

Network Upgrades: Technological upgrades and forks in a cryptocurrency's underlying blockchain can influence its price. Ethereum's shift to Proof of Stake (PoS) from Proof of Work (PoW), for instance, has major implications for the value of ETH.

Supply and Demand: Like any asset, cryptocurrency prices are affected by the basic laws of supply and demand. Bitcoin's fixed supply (capped at 21 million coins) often leads to price increases when demand surges.

Institutional Investment: The entry of institutional players into the crypto space, through vehicles like Bitcoin ETFs and futures, can drive up prices by increasing liquidity and credibility.

Regulation: Regulatory developments, such as government crackdowns or new legal frameworks, can have a significant impact on crypto prices. Positive regulation tends to boost prices, while restrictive measures can trigger price declines.

EXAMPLE: TRADING BITCOIN FUTURES

Let's say you expect Bitcoin's price to increase due to a favorable regulatory development. You decide to go long on a Bitcoin futures contract that represents 1 Bitcoin, with a futures price of $40,000.

Scenario 1: Bitcoin's price rises to $45,000. You close your position and profit from the $5,000 price difference.

Scenario 2: Bitcoin's price falls to $35,000. You close your position to limit your loss, taking a $5,000 hit on the contract.

In both cases, your profit or loss is determined by the difference between the futures contract price and the spot price at the time of closing.

STRATEGIES FOR TRADING CRYPTO FUTURES

There are several strategies traders use to profit from crypto futures. Some of the most common include:

Long/Short Positions: Traders can go long if they expect the price of the cryptocurrency to rise, or short if they expect a price drop.

Hedging: Investors can use futures to hedge against price drops in their cryptocurrency holdings. By taking a short position in futures, you can offset potential losses in your spot crypto assets.

Arbitrage: Some traders take advantage of price discrepancies between different exchanges or between spot and futures prices through arbitrage strategies.

Scalping and Day Trading: Due to the high volatility of crypto, scalpers and day traders often aim to profit from small price movements over short timeframes.

RISKS OF TRADING CRYPTO FUTURES

As with any financial instrument, trading crypto futures comes with risks:

Volatility: Cryptocurrencies are known for their extreme price swings. While this volatility creates opportunities for profit, it also increases the likelihood of significant losses, particularly when trading on margin.

Leverage Risk: The high leverage offered in crypto futures can amplify both gains and losses, meaning traders can lose more than their initial investment if the market moves against them.

Regulatory Risk: The cryptocurrency space is still evolving, and regulatory actions by governments around the world can impact the value and legality of cryptocurrency trading.

Counterparty Risk: Trading crypto futures on unregulated or less reputable platforms increases the risk of platform failure, hacks, or fraud.

Trading crypto futures is a high-risk, high-reward endeavor that requires an understanding of the unique dynamics of the cryptocurrency market. With the right strategies and risk management, traders can capitalize on the volatility and rapid price movements in the digital asset space.

In the next chapter, we'll explore Trading Index Futures, where you'll learn how futures contracts based on major market indices like the S&P 500 or Nasdaq 100 can be used for both speculation and hedging in traditional financial markets.

28: TRADING INDEX FUTURES

I ndex futures are a key part of the futures trading landscape, providing traders with a way to speculate on or hedge against the performance of entire stock market indices rather than individual stocks. These instruments offer exposure to a basket of securities through a single contract, making them an attractive tool for both institutional and retail traders. In this chapter, we'll explore how index futures work, why they are traded, and strategies for successful trading.

WHAT ARE INDEX FUTURES?

Index futures are futures contracts that derive their value from the performance of a particular stock market index. These contracts allow traders to bet on the direction of the underlying index, such as the S&P 500, Nasdaq 100, Dow Jones Industrial Average, or international indices like the FTSE 100 and DAX 30.

When you trade index futures, you are speculating on the future value of the index at the contract's expiration. Since these futures are cash-settled, no physical assets are exchanged. Instead, your profit or loss is based on the difference between the contract's purchase price and the index's value at the time the contract is settled.

POPULAR INDEX FUTURES

Some of the most commonly traded index futures include:

S&P 500 Futures (ES): Tracks the performance of the top 500 U.S. companies, making it one of the most widely traded index futures in the world. Traders use it to speculate on the overall performance of the U.S. stock market.

Nasdaq 100 Futures (NQ): Represents the 100 largest non-financial companies listed on the Nasdaq exchange, primarily covering technology and growth stocks. It's popular among those focusing on tech-heavy industries.

Dow Jones Industrial Average Futures (YM): Tracks 30 of the largest blue-chip stocks in the U.S. economy. This index is often considered a gauge of broad economic health.

Russell 2000 Futures (RTY): Focuses on small-cap U.S. companies. Traders use it to gain exposure to the performance of smaller, domestically focused businesses.

FTSE 100 Futures (Z): Represents the largest companies listed on the London Stock Exchange, providing a way to trade the overall performance of the U.K. stock market.

DAX 30 Futures (FDAX): Tracks the top 30 German companies listed on the Frankfurt Stock Exchange and serves as a key indicator of the European economy.

WHY TRADE INDEX FUTURES?

Index futures offer several advantages for traders and investors:

Diversification: Since index futures represent a broad market or sector, they provide diversified exposure, reducing the risk associated with trading individual stocks.

Hedging: Index futures are often used by investors to hedge against declines in their equity portfolios. For example, a long-term investor can use short index futures to protect against potential losses in their stock holdings during market downturns.

Leverage: Like other futures contracts, index futures allow traders to control large positions with a smaller amount of capital, amplifying potential profits (and losses).

Liquidity: Index futures, particularly those based on major indices like the S&P 500 and Nasdaq 100, are highly liquid. This ensures tight bid-ask spreads and allows for efficient execution of trades.

Speculation: Index futures allow traders to speculate on the overall direction of the market or a specific sector, enabling them to profit from both rising and falling markets.

HOW INDEX FUTURES WORK

Index futures work similarly to other types of futures contracts, with some key elements to understand:

Contract Specifications: Each index futures contract has specific details, including the size of the contract, the tick size (the smallest price movement), and the index it tracks. For example, one S&P 500 futures contract represents 50 times the index value.

Settlement: Most index futures are cash-settled, meaning there's no physical delivery of stocks. Instead, the difference between the futures price and the index price at expiration is paid in cash.

Leverage: Index futures offer significant leverage, meaning traders can control large amounts of capital with a relatively small initial margin. However, this also increases the risk of significant losses.

Expiration: Index futures have specific expiration dates, usually quarterly (March, June, September, and December). Traders can choose to hold their positions until expiration or roll them over to a new contract.

EXAMPLE: TRADING S&P 500 FUTURES

Let's say you believe the U.S. stock market will rise in the near future. You decide to buy an S&P 500 futures contract at 4,000 points, and each point is worth $50.

Scenario 1: The index rises to 4,100 points by the time you close your position. You would make 100 points of profit, which equates to 100 × $50 = $5,000.

Scenario 2: The index falls to 3,900 points. You would lose 100 points, resulting in a loss of $5,000.

In both cases, your profit or loss is calculated based on the difference between the contract price and the index's value at settlement or when the position is closed.

FACTORS INFLUENCING INDEX PRICES

Several factors influence the value of indices and, in turn, index futures prices:

Macroeconomic Data: Economic indicators such as GDP growth, unemployment figures, inflation rates, and consumer confidence reports can significantly impact index prices.

Interest Rates: Central bank policies and interest rate changes can drive market sentiment and affect the valuation of stocks within an index. Rising interest rates typically weigh on stock prices, while lower rates can be supportive.

Corporate Earnings: Since indices like the S&P 500 are composed of individual companies, quarterly earnings reports can drive significant movements in index prices. Strong earnings lead to upward momentum, while weak earnings can trigger declines.

Market Sentiment: Investor sentiment, often influenced by geopolitical events, market news, or government policies, can sway the overall direction of an index.

Sector Performance: Indices are composed of different sectors (technology, healthcare, financials, etc.). A surge or decline in a particular sector can impact the entire index. For example, tech stocks heavily influence the Nasdaq 100.

STRATEGIES FOR TRADING INDEX FUTURES

Several strategies can be employed to trade index futures successfully:

Directional Trading: Traders can take long or short positions based on their expectations of the market's direction. Going long profits from rising prices, while shorting profits from falling prices.

Hedging: Investors can use index futures to hedge their stock portfolios. If you're concerned about a market downturn, you can short index futures to offset potential losses in your stock holdings.

Spread Trading: Traders may engage in **spread trading**, which involves taking long and short positions in different index futures contracts, such as going long on the Nasdaq 100 while shorting the S&P 500 to exploit relative performance differences between indices.

Scalping and Day Trading: Due to the high liquidity of index futures, many traders focus on short-term strategies, making small, frequent trades to capture quick price movements.

RISKS OF TRADING INDEX FUTURES

As with all trading, index futures come with inherent risks:

Leverage Risk: While leverage can amplify profits, it also increases the potential for significant losses. Traders can lose more than their initial margin if the market moves sharply against them.

Market Risk: Index prices can be affected by a wide range of unpredictable factors, including geopolitical events, natural disasters, and sudden changes in government policies.

Liquidity Risk: While major index futures are highly liquid, smaller or international index futures may experience lower liquidity, leading to wider spreads and slippage in trade execution.

Overnight Risk: Since index futures trade nearly 24/7, positions held overnight or over the weekend are exposed to global market events and news, which can cause sharp price movements when the markets reopen.

Trading index futures provides an efficient and leveraged way to speculate on the overall performance of financial markets or hedge against potential declines. By understanding the mechanics, strategies, and risks involved, traders can make informed decisions and potentially profit from market trends.

In the next chapter, we'll dive into Trading Interest Rate Futures, where we will explore how traders use these contracts to bet on or hedge against changes in interest rates and the bond market.

29: TRADING INTEREST RATE FUTURES

I nterest rate futures provide a way for traders to speculate on or hedge against changes in interest rates, often linked to government bonds or short-term interest rates. These futures are essential for investors who want to manage interest rate risk, and they are widely used by both institutional and retail traders. In this chapter, we'll explore what interest rate futures are, how they work, popular contracts, and strategies for trading them.

WHAT ARE INTEREST RATE FUTURES?

Interest rate futures are standardized futures contracts where the underlying asset is typically a debt instrument such as government bonds or a specific interest rate, such as the Eurodollar rate, U.S. Treasury yields, or LIBOR (London Interbank Offered Rate). These futures allow traders to speculate on the future movement of interest rates. Since bond prices and interest rates move inversely, when interest rates rise, bond prices fall and vice versa.

Rather than taking physical delivery of bonds, interest rate futures are cash-settled, and traders are compensated based on the difference between the contract price and the final settlement price.

POPULAR INTEREST RATE FUTURES CONTRACTS

Some of the most commonly traded interest rate futures contracts include:

Eurodollar Futures: These are some of the most liquid futures contracts in the world. They track the expected U.S. dollar interest rate for 90-day deposits outside the U.S. (Eurodollars). Traders use these futures to hedge against or speculate on changes in short-term interest rates.

U.S. Treasury Bond Futures: These contracts track the prices of U.S. Treasury bonds. The most popular ones include the 2-year, 5-year, 10-year, and 30-year Treasury bond futures. Investors use these contracts to hedge against changes in long-term interest rates or speculate on the future direction of interest rates.

Federal Funds Rate Futures: These futures track the U.S. Federal Reserve's target federal funds rate. They are commonly used by institutions to manage short-term interest rate exposure or to speculate on the Fed's future interest rate decisions.

LIBOR Futures: LIBOR futures track the London Interbank Offered Rate, which is a key benchmark for short-term interest rates globally. Despite LIBOR being phased out, it remains a significant part of interest rate trading until fully replaced by new benchmarks like **SOFR** (Secured Overnight Financing Rate).

HOW INTEREST RATE FUTURES WORK

Interest rate futures work similarly to other futures contracts but are influenced by changes in interest rates and bond yields. Here's a brief overview of their mechanics:

Contract Specifications: Each interest rate futures contract specifies the interest rate it tracks, the contract size, and the duration. For example, a U.S. Treasury bond futures contract might track the price of $100,000 worth of U.S. Treasury bonds with a maturity of 10 years.

Pricing: The price of an interest rate future reflects market expectations of future interest rate levels. As interest rates rise, the price of the futures contract typically falls.

Cash Settlement: Like most financial futures, interest rate futures are cash-settled. This means no actual bonds or financial instruments are delivered. Instead, the buyer or seller of the contract receives the difference between the contract price and the final settlement price.

Leverage: Like other futures, interest rate futures offer leverage, meaning you can control a large position with a relatively small amount of capital. However, leverage increases the risk of losses, especially in volatile markets.

WHY TRADE INTEREST RATE FUTURES?

Interest rate futures are popular for several reasons, offering unique advantages to both speculators and hedgers:

Hedging Interest Rate Risk: Businesses, banks, and investors use interest rate futures to hedge against changes in interest rates that can affect their financial operations. For example, a company with a large amount of floating-rate debt may use interest rate futures to lock in current interest rates and protect against future increases.

Speculation: Traders can speculate on future movements in interest rates, profiting from their ability to predict changes in central bank policy, inflation trends, or bond market fluctuations.

Diversification: Interest rate futures provide a way to diversify portfolios. Since interest rates often move inversely to stock markets, these futures can act as a hedge in a broader investment strategy.

Liquidity: Major interest rate futures, especially Eurodollar and U.S. Treasury bond futures, are highly liquid, making it easy to enter and exit trades with tight bid-ask spreads.

EXAMPLE: TRADING 10-YEAR U.S. TREASURY BOND FUTURES

Let's say you believe that the U.S. Federal Reserve will raise interest rates in the coming months, leading to a decrease in U.S. Treasury bond prices. You decide to short (sell) a 10-Year U.S. Treasury bond futures contract currently priced at 132-16 (or 132.5).

Scenario 1: If interest rates rise as expected and the bond price falls to 130-00 (or 130.0), you make a profit. The price difference is 132.5 - 130.0 = 2.5 points. For a standard contract where each point is worth $1,000, you would make 2.5 × $1,000 = $2,500.

Scenario 2: If interest rates fall instead and bond prices rise to 134-00, you incur a loss. The price difference is 134.0 - 132.5 = 1.5 points, resulting in a loss of 1.5 × $1,000 = $1,500.

FACTORS AFFECTING INTEREST RATE FUTURES

Several factors influence the prices of interest rate futures:

Central Bank Policies: Decisions by central banks, such as the U.S. Federal Reserve, European Central Bank, or Bank of England, to raise or lower interest rates directly impact interest rate futures. Futures markets often react to central bank statements and economic forecasts.

Inflation: Rising inflation typically leads to higher interest rates as central banks attempt to control inflation. Inflation expectations can influence bond yields and interest rate futures pricing.

Economic Data: Key economic indicators, such as employment reports, GDP growth, and consumer spending, affect interest rate expectations. Strong economic data may push rates higher, while weak data may lower rates.

Market Sentiment: Investor sentiment regarding the broader economy, geopolitical risks, and global financial stability can also impact interest rate futures prices. Risk-averse environments often lead to falling interest rates as investors flock to safe assets like bonds.

STRATEGIES FOR TRADING INTEREST RATE FUTURES

Several strategies can be employed when trading interest rate futures:

Hedging: Corporations, financial institutions, and portfolio managers use interest rate futures to hedge their exposure to rising or falling interest rates. For example, an investor holding a portfolio of bonds might short U.S. Treasury futures to protect against rising interest rates.

Spread Trading: Spread traders may trade the difference between two interest rate futures contracts. For example, you might go long on short-term Eurodollar futures while shorting longer-term Treasury futures, betting that the yield curve will flatten or steepen.

Directional Trading: Traders can take a directional position, going long if they expect rates to fall (bond prices to rise) or short if they expect rates to rise (bond prices to fall). This approach is often based on economic forecasts, central bank policies, or inflation expectations.

Arbitrage: Sophisticated traders may look for arbitrage opportunities between different interest rate instruments, such as trading futures against actual bond prices to exploit pricing inefficiencies.

RISKS OF TRADING INTEREST RATE FUTURES

Trading interest rate futures comes with several risks:

Leverage Risk: The use of leverage can amplify both profits and losses. Sudden changes in interest rate expectations or central bank actions can lead to large price swings, resulting in substantial gains or losses.

Economic Uncertainty: Economic data can be unpredictable, and unexpected results can lead to significant market movements. For example, surprise inflation reports or changes in employment data can trigger sharp interest rate moves.

Political and Geopolitical Risks: Government policies, fiscal decisions, or geopolitical tensions can affect market sentiment and, in turn, interest rate futures prices.

Liquidity Risk: While major interest rate futures are liquid, smaller or less commonly traded contracts may experience lower liquidity, leading to wider bid-ask spreads and potential slippage during trade execution.

Trading interest rate futures offers an effective way to manage interest rate risk, hedge bond portfolios, or speculate on changes in interest rates. By understanding how these contracts work, the factors that influence interest rates, and the strategies involved, traders can effectively navigate this dynamic market.

In the next section, we will delve into sophisticated strategies that can enhance your trading performance, including spread trading, options on futures, and automated trading systems.

PART 8: ADVANCED TRADING TECHNIQUES

30: SPREAD TRADING: CALENDAR SPREADS AND INTERMARKET SPREADS

S pread trading is a popular strategy in the futures market that involves simultaneously buying and selling two related futures contracts to profit from the price difference between them. In this chapter, we will focus on two common types of spread trading: calendar spreads and intermarket spreads.

We will explore the mechanics of these spreads, their advantages, and considerations for implementing them in your trading strategy.

CALENDAR SPREADS

A calendar spread, also known as a time or horizontal spread, involves buying and selling futures contracts of the same underlying asset but with different expiration dates. Traders take advantage of the price difference between the near-month (current month) and far-month (future month) contracts. The goal is to profit from changes in the price relationship between the two contracts over time.

1. MECHANICS OF CALENDAR SPREADS

In a calendar spread, a trader can take a long or short position. Let's consider the following example:

Long Calendar Spread: A trader buys the near-month contract and simultaneously sells the far-month contract. The expectation is that the price of the near-month contract will increase or the price of the far-month contract will decrease, resulting in a favorable price difference between the two contracts.

Short Calendar Spread: A trader sells the near-month contract and simultaneously buys the far-month contract. The expectation is that the price of the near-month contract will decrease or the price of the far-month contract will increase, resulting in a favorable price difference.

The profitability of a calendar spread depends on the price movement and the time decay of the contracts involved. Traders aim to capture the spread's maximum value as the expiration date of the near-month contract approaches.

2. ADVANTAGES OF CALENDAR SPREADS

Calendar spreads offer several advantages:

Reduced Exposure to Spot Price Movements: Calendar spreads can be less susceptible to abrupt spot price fluctuations compared to outright futures positions. The strategy relies more on the price difference between contracts than the absolute price direction.

Lower Margin Requirements: Calendar spreads typically require lower margin requirements than outright futures positions. This can provide cost efficiencies and make the strategy more accessible to traders.

Time Decay Opportunities: Traders can benefit from time decay in calendar spreads. As the near-month contract approaches expiration, the spread's value can increase if the price relationship between the two contracts moves favorably.

3. CONSIDERATIONS FOR CALENDAR SPREADS

When implementing calendar spreads, consider the following:

Contract Selection: Choose futures contracts with appropriate liquidity and sufficient price volatility to maximize trading opportunities.

Market Analysis: Conduct thorough market analysis to identify potential price trends or factors that may impact the price relationship between the near-month and far-month contracts.

Time Horizon: Determine the optimal holding period for the spread. Some traders may prefer shorter-term spreads, while others may hold positions until expiration approaches.

INTERMARKET SPREADS

Intermarket spreads, also known as relative value spreads, involve trading futures contracts of related but different markets. Traders seek to profit from the price relationship between the two markets. Intermarket spreads can be implemented between different commodities, different contract months of the same commodity, or even different futures exchanges.

1. MECHANICS OF INTERMARKET SPREADS

Intermarket spreads can be executed as either a long or short position.

Long Intermarket Spread: A trader takes a long position in one futures contract and a short position in another related futures contract. The expectation is that the long position will outperform the short position, resulting in a profit from the price difference between the two contracts.

Short Intermarket Spread: A trader takes a short position in one futures contract and a long position in another related futures contract. The expectation is that the short position will outperform the long position, leading to a profit from the price difference.

The profitability of an intermarket spread depends on the price relationship between the two markets involved. Traders analyze factors such as supply and demand dynamics, market interdependencies, and macroeconomic factors to identify opportunities for intermarket spreads.

2. ADVANTAGES OF INTERMARKET SPREADS

Intermarket spreads offer several advantages:

Diversification: By trading different markets, traders can diversify their exposure and reduce the risk associated with a single asset or market. Intermarket spreads can provide a more balanced approach to trading.

Risk Management: Intermarket spreads can help manage risk by offsetting potential losses in one market with gains in another. This can provide a hedge against adverse market movements.

Profit Opportunities: Intermarket spreads allow traders to capture price discrepancies or misalignments between related markets. By identifying markets that are temporarily overvalued or undervalued, traders can profit from their convergence.

3. CONSIDERATIONS FOR INTERMARKET SPREADS

When implementing intermarket spreads, consider the following:

Market Correlation: Analyze the correlation between the two markets involved in the spread. A strong positive or negative correlation enhances the likelihood of profitable spread trading.

Market Analysis: Conduct thorough analysis of both markets to identify factors that may impact their price relationship. Consider supply and demand fundamentals, economic indicators, geopolitical events, and other market-specific factors.

Margin and Leverage: Understand the margin requirements and leverage associated with the futures contracts involved in the intermarket spread. Proper risk management and position sizing are crucial.

Spread trading offers traders opportunities to profit from the price differences between related futures contracts or markets. Calendar spreads capitalize on time decay and the price relationship between near-month and far-month contracts.

Intermarket spreads allow traders to benefit from price discrepancies between different markets. By understanding the mechanics, advantages, and considerations of calendar spreads and intermarket spreads, traders can incorporate these strategies into their trading arsenal.

In the next chapter, we'll dive into how options work within the futures landscape and explore strategies that allow you to manage risk, leverage positions, and take advantage of various market conditions.

31: OPTIONS ON FUTURES

INTRODUCTION AND STRATEGIES

Options on futures are derivative contracts that give traders the right, but not the obligation, to buy or sell a futures contract at a predetermined price (the strike price) on or before a specific date (the expiration date).

In this chapter, we will provide an introduction to options on futures and explore various strategies that traders can employ to enhance their trading approach.

UNDERSTANDING OPTIONS ON FUTURES

Options on futures offer traders additional flexibility and risk management tools in the futures market. By trading options, traders can profit from price movements, hedge against potential losses, and gain exposure to market volatility.

Call Options: A call option on a futures contract gives the holder the right to buy the underlying futures contract at the strike price before the expiration date. Traders typically buy call options when they expect the price of the underlying futures contract to rise.

Put Options: A put option on a futures contract gives the holder the right to sell the underlying futures contract at the strike price before the expiration date. Traders usually purchase put options when they anticipate the price of the underlying futures contract to decline.

OPTIONS TRADING STRATEGIES

There are various strategies that traders can employ when trading options on futures. These strategies provide traders with different ways to manage risk, profit from price movements, or generate income. Here are a few commonly used strategies:

1. BUYING CALL OR PUT OPTIONS

Options Trading: transworld-fp7.eu

Traders can purchase call options if they anticipate a bullish market outlook or put options if they expect a bearish market outlook. Buying options provides traders with leveraged exposure to price movements with limited risk, as the maximum loss is limited to the premium paid for the option.

2. SELLING CALL OR PUT OPTIONS

Selling call options, also known as writing call options, involves taking on the obligation to sell the underlying futures contract at the strike price if the option is exercised. Conversely, selling put options, or writing put options, entails the obligation to buy the underlying futures contract at the strike price if the option is exercised. Traders who sell options aim to collect the premium and benefit from the time decay of the options.

3. SPREADS

Options spreads involve simultaneously buying and selling multiple options to take advantage of price differentials and reduce risk. Common types of spreads include:

Bull Call Spread: Buying a lower strike call option and simultaneously selling a higher strike call option to profit from a moderate upward price movement.

Bear Put Spread: Buying a higher strike put option and simultaneously selling a lower strike put option to profit from a moderate downward price movement.

Iron Condor: Combining a bull put spread and a bear call spread to profit from a range-bound market where the price remains between the two strike prices.

4. STRADDLES AND STRANGLES

Straddles and strangles involve simultaneously buying both a call and a put option (straddle) or multiple call and put options with different strike prices (strangle). These strategies are used when traders expect significant price volatility but are unsure about the direction of the price movement.

RISK MANAGEMENT AND CONSIDERATIONS

When trading options on futures, it's crucial to consider risk management and account for factors such as time decay, implied volatility, and market conditions. Proper position sizing, setting stop-loss orders, and understanding the potential profit and loss scenarios are vital for successful options trading.

Options on futures provide traders with additional tools and strategies to navigate the futures market. By understanding the basics of options trading and employing various strategies, traders can tailor their approach to their market outlook and risk tolerance. Whether it's buying or selling options, utilizing spreads, or implementing straddles and strangles, options on futures offer a versatile range of opportunities.

It's important to note that options trading involves inherent risks, including the potential loss of the premium paid for the options. Traders should thoroughly understand the mechanics and nuances of options on futures before entering into trades. Risk management strategies, such as setting stop-loss orders and diversifying positions, are essential for mitigating potential losses.

Furthermore, keeping track of market conditions, implied volatility, and staying up to date with relevant news and events can provide valuable insights for options trading decisions. Regularly reassessing and adjusting strategies based on market dynamics is a prudent approach to maximize profitability and minimize risk.

In the next chapter, Automated Trading and Algorithmic Strategies, we will dive into the world of algorithmic trading and the use of automation to execute trades more effectively.

32: AUTOMATED TRADING AND ALGORITHMIC STRATEGIES

In recent years, technological advancements have revolutionized the way financial markets operate. One notable development is the rise of automated trading and algorithmic strategies. In this chapter, we will explore the concept of automated trading, discuss algorithmic strategies, and delve into the benefits and considerations of implementing these approaches in futures trading.

UNDERSTANDING AUTOMATED TRADING

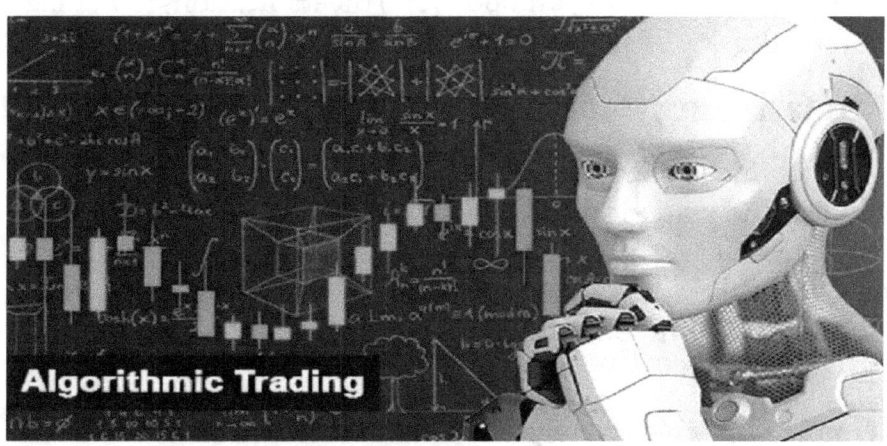

Algorithmic Trading: businesspost.ng

Automated trading, also known as algorithmic trading or algo-trading, refers to the use of computer programs or algorithms to execute trading orders. These algorithms are designed to analyze market data, identify trading opportunities, and automatically execute trades based on predefined rules and parameters.

Components of Automated Trading

Automated trading systems typically consist of the following components:

Data Feed: Market data, including price quotes, trade volumes, and other relevant information, is fed into the trading system. This data forms the basis for analysis and decision-making.

Trading Algorithm: The algorithm is the core component of the automated trading system. It processes the market data, applies predefined rules and strategies, and generates trade signals.

Order Execution: Once trade signals are generated, the automated trading system automatically sends orders to the exchange or broker for execution.

Risk Management: Automated trading systems often incorporate risk management mechanisms, such as setting stop-loss orders, position sizing, and portfolio diversification, to manage potential risks.

ALGORITHMIC TRADING STRATEGIES

Algorithmic trading strategies are based on mathematical models and statistical analysis of historical and real-time market data. These strategies aim to capitalize on market inefficiencies, price patterns, or other factors to generate trading signals.

Here are some common algorithmic trading strategies:

Trend-Following Strategies: Trend-following strategies aim to identify and capitalize on market trends. These algorithms analyze price movements and technical indicators to determine the direction of the trend and generate buy or sell signals.

Mean Reversion Strategies: Mean reversion strategies assume that prices tend to revert to their average or historical values. Algorithms employing mean reversion strategies identify over-bought or oversold conditions and generate trade signals based on the expectation of price correction.

Arbitrage Strategies: Arbitrage strategies aim to exploit price discrepancies between different markets or related instruments. Algorithms scan multiple markets, identify price differentials, and execute trades to profit from the temporary mispricing.

Statistical Arbitrage Strategies: Statistical arbitrage strategies rely on statistical analysis and modeling to identify relation-ships between securities or markets. Algorithms identify devi-ations from historical relationships and generate trades based on the expectation of the relationship reverting to its mean.

BENEFITS OF AUTOMATED TRADING AND ALGORITHMIC STRATEGIES

Implementing automated trading and algorithmic strategies can offer several benefits:

Speed and Efficiency: Automated trading systems can execute trades at high speeds, enabling traders to capitalize on fleeting market opportunities and minimize slippage.

Consistency: Algorithms follow predefined rules and strategies consistently, removing the impact of emotional and impulsive decision-making that can affect manual trading.

Backtesting and Optimization: Algorithms can be backtested using historical data to assess their performance. This allows traders to refine and optimize strategies before deploying them in live trading.

Diversification: Automated trading systems can handle mul-tiple instruments and markets simultaneously, enabling traders to diversify their portfolios and spread risk.

CONSIDERATIONS FOR AUTOMATED TRADING

While automated trading offers numerous advantages, there are important considerations to keep in mind:

System Reliability: The reliability of the automated trading system is crucial. It should be built on robust infrastructure and undergo rigorous testing to ensure it functions properly under various market conditions.

Risk Management: Automated trading systems should incorporate effective risk management measures. Traders must define and implement appropriate risk controls, such as setting stop-loss orders, managing position sizes, and diversifying strategies. It's essential to monitor risk exposure and adjust risk parameters as needed.

Market Monitoring: Automated trading systems still require monitoring to ensure they are functioning correctly and adapting to changing market conditions. Traders should regularly review performance, analyze results, and make necessary adjustments.

Risk of Technical Glitches: Automated trading systems are reliant on technology, and there is a risk of technical glitches or system failures. Traders should have contingency plans in place and consider implementing safeguards, such as redundancy and backup systems.

Over-Optimization: While backtesting and optimization are valuable tools, there is a risk of over-optimizing strategies based on historical data. Traders should be cautious not to create strategies that are too tailored to past market conditions, as they may not perform as expected in live trading.

Regulatory Considerations: Traders engaging in automated trading should be aware of and comply with applicable regulatory requirements and guidelines. Certain jurisdictions may have specific rules or restrictions on automated trading activities.

Constant Learning and Adaptation: Markets evolve, and trading strategies need to adapt accordingly. Traders should continuously educate themselves, stay updated on market trends, and be willing to adjust their algorithms and strategies as needed.

Automated trading and algorithmic strategies have transformed the landscape of futures trading, providing traders with speed, efficiency, and consistency.

These approaches offer benefits such as increased trading opportunities, improved risk management, and enhanced portfolio diversification. However, they also require careful consideration of system reliability, ongoing monitoring, and effective risk management practices.

Successful implementation of automated trading and algorithmic strategies requires a blend of technical expertise, market knowledge, and risk management skills.

Traders should approach these strategies with proper planning, testing, and an understanding of the potential benefits and risks involved.

In the next section, we will focus on how to structure your trading approach, set clear goals, assess your risk tolerance, and maintain the discipline needed to stay on course.

PART 9: DEVELOPING A TRADING PLAN

33: GOAL SETTING AND RISK TOLERANCE ASSESSMENT

Successful futures trading requires a clear understanding of your goals and risk tolerance. In this chapter, we will explore the importance of goal setting and risk tolerance assessment, and how they can help you develop a tailored trading plan to achieve your objectives.

SETTING TRADING GOALS

Setting clear and realistic trading goals is essential for guiding your trading activities. Goals provide a sense of direction and purpose, helping you stay focused and motivated. When setting trading goals, consider the following:

Define Your Financial Objectives: Identify your financial objectives, such as capital preservation, income generation, capital growth, or a specific target return on investment. Clarify your desired outcome and timeframe for achieving your financial goals.

Determine Your Trading Style and Time Commitment: Consider your preferred trading style, whether it's day trading, swing trading, or longer-term position trading. Assess the amount of time you can dedicate to trading, taking into account your other commitments and responsibilities.

Assess Risk Appetite: Understand your risk appetite and tolerance for potential losses. This involves considering your financial situation, risk capacity, and psychological comfort with taking risks. A realistic assessment of your risk tolerance will guide your trading decisions and help you manage risk effectively.

Set Measurable and Realistic Goals: Make your trading goals specific, measurable, achievable, relevant, and time-bound (SMART). For example, instead of aiming to "make a lot of money," set a specific monthly profit target or a target annual return on investment that aligns with your risk tolerance and trading style.

RISK TOLERANCE ASSESSMENT

Assessing your risk tolerance is crucial for determining the level of risk you are comfortable with in your trading activities. Here are key factors to consider:

Financial Situation and Capital: Evaluate your financial situation, including your available capital, income sources, and expenses. Determine the portion of your capital that you are willing to allocate to futures trading and consider the potential impact of losses on your overall financial well-being.

Time Horizon: Assess your time horizon for achieving your trading goals. A longer time horizon may allow for a more aggressive approach, while a shorter time horizon may require a more conservative strategy to manage risk.

Risk Capacity: Consider your risk capacity, which refers to the amount of risk you can afford to take based on your financial situation, income stability, and available resources. Assessing risk capacity helps ensure that you don't overextend yourself or take on excessive risk.

Risk Tolerance and Emotional Resilience: Evaluate your risk tolerance and emotional resilience in relation to potential losses. Consider your psychological comfort with market fluctuations, drawdowns, and the possibility of losing a portion of your trading capital. Being aware of your emotional response to risk can help you make objective trading decisions.

INCORPORATING GOALS AND RISK TOLERANCE IN YOUR TRADING PLAN

Once you have established your trading goals and assessed your risk tolerance, it's important to integrate them into your trading plan. Your trading plan should outline your strategies, risk management techniques, position sizing guidelines, and the criteria for evaluating and adjusting your trades.

Aligning Strategies with Goals: Ensure that your trading strategies align with your goals and risk tolerance. For example, if capital preservation is your primary goal, you may opt for more conservative strategies with lower risk exposure. If capital growth is your objective, you might consider strategies that have the potential for higher returns, but also come with higher risk.

Risk Management: Integrate risk management techniques into your trading plan to protect your capital and minimize potential losses. Determine appropriate stop-loss levels for each trade, implement position sizing rules, and consider diversifying your portfolio across different instruments or asset classes.

Regular Evaluation and Adjustment: Regularly review and evaluate your trading performance against your goals. Assess whether your strategies are effective and align with your risk tolerance. Be open to adjusting your trading plan as needed to stay on track with your objectives.

EMBRACING FLEXIBILITY

Goal setting and risk tolerance assessment are not static processes. As your financial situation, market conditions, and personal circumstances change, it's essential to reassess and adjust your goals and risk tolerance accordingly. Flexibility allows you to adapt to evolving market dynamics and optimize your trading approach.

SEEKING PROFESSIONAL GUIDANCE

If you are unsure about setting goals or assessing your risk tolerance, consider seeking guidance from a qualified financial professional or trading mentor. They can provide insights, help you evaluate your risk profile, and offer valuable advice on aligning your trading goals with your risk tolerance.

Goal setting and risk tolerance assessment are crucial steps in developing a successful futures trading plan. Clearly defining your trading objectives, understanding your risk tolerance, and integrating them into your trading strategy can enhance your decision-making process and improve your chances of achieving long-term success.

Regularly review and adjust your goals and risk tolerance as necessary, and consider seeking professional guidance to optimize your trading approach.

In the next chapter, we will focus on how to create a personalized, robust strategy that integrates your market insights, risk management practices, and trading style.

34: BUILDING A TRADING STRATEGY

A well-defined and robust trading strategy is essential for achieving consistent success in futures trading. In this chapter, we will guide you through the process of building a trading strategy that aligns with your goals, risk tolerance, and market conditions.

DEFINING YOUR TRADING OBJECTIVES AND STYLE

Begin by clearly defining your trading objectives. Are you seeking short-term profits or long-term capital growth? Do you prefer day trading, swing trading, or position trading? Understanding your objectives and preferred trading style will guide the development of your strategy.

MARKET ANALYSIS AND RESEARCH

Conduct thorough market analysis and research to gain insights into the instruments you wish to trade. Understand the underlying factors influencing price movements, such as supply and demand dynamics, economic indicators, geopolitical events, and market sentiment. Use both fundamental and technical analysis to identify potential trading opportunities.

ENTRY AND EXIT CRITERIA

Develop clear and objective entry and exit criteria for your trades. Determine the indicators or signals that will trigger your entry into a trade, such as breakouts, moving averages, or trend reversals. Similarly, establish criteria for exiting a trade, including profit targets and stop-loss levels to manage risk.

RISK MANAGEMENT

Integrate risk management principles into your trading strategy. Set appropriate position sizing rules based on your risk tolerance and the characteristics of each trade. Determine your maximum acceptable risk per trade and implement stop-loss orders to limit potential losses. Regularly review and adjust your risk management parameters as needed.

TESTING AND OPTIMIZATION

Before implementing your trading strategy in live trading, test it thoroughly using historical data. Backtesting allows you to evaluate the performance of your strategy under various market conditions. Make adjustments to your strategy based on the results of backtesting and optimize it for improved performance.

RECORD-KEEPING AND PERFORMANCE EVALUATION

Maintain a detailed trading journal to record your trades, including entry and exit points, trade rationale, and outcomes. Regularly evaluate your trading performance by reviewing your journal. Identify strengths and weaknesses in your strategy and make necessary adjustments to enhance your future trading decisions.

ADAPTING TO CHANGING MARKET CONDITIONS

Recognize that markets are dynamic, and strategies that were successful in the past may require adjustments to remain effective. Continuously monitor market conditions, stay updated on economic and geopolitical developments, and be prepared to adapt your strategy to changing circumstances.

CONTINUOUS LEARNING AND IMPROVEMENT

Futures trading is a constant learning process. Stay informed about new trading techniques, market trends, and technological advancements that may impact your strategy. Engage in ongoing education, attend webinars or seminars, and seek insights from experienced traders to enhance your knowledge and improve your strategy.

BACKTESTING AND FORWARD TESTING

Regularly backtest your trading strategy using historical data to ensure its viability and profitability. Additionally, forward testing, or paper trading, can provide valuable insights by implementing your strategy in real-time without risking actual capital. Monitor the performance of your strategy during forward testing and make any necessary refinements.

Building a trading strategy is a crucial step towards achieving success in futures trading. By defining your trading objectives, conducting thorough market analysis, establishing clear entry and exit criteria, implementing effective risk management, testing and optimizing your strategy, and continuously learning and adapting, you can develop a strategy that aligns with your goals and helps you navigate the dynamic nature of the futures market.

Remember to maintain a trading journal, regularly evaluate your performance, and make necessary adjustments to enhance your strategy. Stay disciplined and patient, as consistency and adaptability are key to long-term success.

In the next chapter, we will explore how to evaluate your strategy using historical data and real-time market conditions.

35: BACKTESTING AND FORWARD TESTING

Backtesting and forward testing are crucial processes in evaluating and refining your trading strategy. In this chapter, we will explore the importance of backtesting and forward testing, how to conduct them effectively, and the insights they provide for improving your trading approach.

UNDERSTANDING BACKTESTING

Backtesting involves applying your trading strategy to historical market data to assess its performance. It allows you to simulate trades and evaluate how your strategy would have fared in the past. The primary goals of backtesting are:

Performance Evaluation: Backtesting enables you to measure the profitability and effectiveness of your strategy. By analyzing historical trade results, you can assess key metrics such as the win rate, profit factor, risk-to-reward ratio, and drawdowns. This evaluation helps you determine if your strategy aligns with your trading goals and if it has the potential for success.

Strategy Refinement: Backtesting provides insights into the strengths and weaknesses of your strategy. By analyzing past trades, you can identify patterns, trends, or market conditions that worked in your favor or posed challenges. This knowledge allows you to refine your strategy, adjusting parameters, entry and exit rules, or risk management techniques to enhance performance.

Risk Assessment: Backtesting helps you understand the risk associated with your strategy. By analyzing historical drawdowns and potential losses, you can assess the risk-reward profile of your trades. This evaluation allows you to optimize position sizing, set appropriate stop-loss levels, and refine risk management parameters to protect your trading capital.

CONDUCTING EFFECTIVE BACKTESTING

To ensure accurate and meaningful backtesting results, follow these key steps:

Define Clear Rules and Parameters: Clearly define the rules of your trading strategy, including entry and exit criteria, indicators, timeframes, and position sizing rules. Establishing specific parameters ensures consistency in applying your strategy to historical data.

Select Relevant Historical Data: Choose a sufficient and relevant sample of historical data to cover various market conditions. Consider different time periods, market environments, and instruments to capture a comprehensive picture of your strategy's performance.

Use Reliable Backtesting Software: Utilize reliable backtesting software that can handle large amounts of data, execute trades according to your strategy's rules, and generate accurate performance metrics. Popular platforms include MetaTrader, TradeStation, and Amibroker, among others.

Account for Transaction Costs and Slippage: Factor in transaction costs, such as commissions and fees, and account for slippage in your backtesting. These real-world considerations can impact the profitability and feasibility of your strategy.

Perform Statistical Analysis: Analyze the results of your backtesting statistically. Look at metrics such as the average trade return, standard deviation, maximum drawdown, and Sharpe ratio to assess risk-adjusted performance. This analysis provides a quantitative understanding of your strategy's strengths and weaknesses.

FORWARD TESTING AND REAL-TIME VALIDATION

Forward testing, also known as paper trading or demo trading, involves implementing your strategy in real-time without risking real capital. This step allows you to validate the performance of your strategy in current market conditions and gain confidence in its effectiveness.

Simulating Real Trades: Execute trades based on your strategy's rules in a simulated trading environment. Record the results and evaluate them against your performance expectations. Keep in mind that forward testing does not guarantee future results but provides valuable insights into how your strategy performs in real-time.

Evaluating Trade Execution and Emotions: Pay attention to the execution of your trades during forward testing. Assess if you can consistently execute trades according to your strategy's rules and if emotions, such as fear or greed, influence your decision-making. This evaluation helps you identify areas for improvement and refine your trading discipline.

Monitoring Performance and Adaptation: Regularly monitor the performance of your strategy during forward testing. Evaluate its consistency, adaptability to changing market conditions, and ability to deliver expected results. Make adjustments as needed to optimize your strategy for live trading.

Backtesting and forward testing are essential components of developing and refining your trading strategy. Backtesting allows you to evaluate past performance, identify strengths and weaknesses, and refine your approach.

Forward testing validates your strategy in real-time, providing insights into execution, emotions, and adaptability. By incorporating these testing processes into your trading journey, you can make informed decisions, improve your strategy's performance, and increase your chances of success.

In the next chapter, we will explore the role that mindset, emotional control, and discipline play in executing your plan consistently. Even the best strategies can fail without the right psychological approach.

36: PSYCHOLOGY AND DISCIPLINE IN FUTURES TRADING

Successful futures trading requires more than just a solid strategy and market knowledge. It also requires a strong understanding of psychology and the ability to maintain discipline in the face of market fluctuations and emotional challenges.

In this chapter, we will explore the key psychological factors that impact trading performance and provide techniques for cultivating a resilient and disciplined mindset.

THE ROLE OF PSYCHOLOGY IN TRADING

Trading is inherently psychological, as it involves making decisions based on uncertain outcomes and managing emotions during market volatility. Understanding and managing the following psychological factors can significantly impact your trading success:

Emotional Control: Emotions, such as fear, greed, and overconfidence, can cloud judgment and lead to impulsive and irrational trading decisions. Developing emotional control and discipline is crucial for making objective and rational choices based on your trading plan.

Patience and Discipline: Patience and discipline are essential virtues in trading. Waiting for the right trade setups, following your predetermined entry and exit rules, and avoiding impulsive decisions are vital for consistent and profitable trading.

Managing Losses: Losses are an inherent part of trading. Managing losses effectively and maintaining a positive mindset after a losing trade is crucial. Accepting losses as part of the trading process and not letting them negatively impact subsequent trading decisions is key to long-term success.

Overcoming Confirmation Bias: Confirmation bias is the tendency to seek information that confirms preexisting beliefs and ignore contradictory evidence. It can lead to biased decision-making and prevent traders from objectively assessing market conditions. Recognizing and actively combating confirmation bias is important for making informed trading decisions.

Handling Success and Failure: Both success and failure can impact a trader's psychology. Handling success with humility and avoiding complacency is important to prevent overconfidence and maintain discipline. Likewise, bouncing back from failure, learning from mistakes, and not letting past losses affect future decisions are crucial for growth and resilience.

TECHNIQUES FOR DEVELOPING A STRONG TRADING MINDSET

To cultivate a strong trading mindset and maintain discipline, consider the following techniques:

Develop a Trading Plan: Create a detailed trading plan that outlines your strategy, risk management rules, and trading goals. Having a plan provides structure and helps you stay focused and disciplined during trading.

Practice Self-Awareness: Develop self-awareness to recognize and manage your emotions while trading. Regularly assess your mindset, identify any emotional biases, and take steps to control them. Techniques like mindfulness and journaling can enhance self-awareness.

Set Realistic Expectations: Maintain realistic expectations about trading outcomes. Understand that trading involves both wins and losses, and focus on the long-term profitability of your strategy. Avoid chasing quick gains or expecting unrealistic returns.

Stick to Your Trading Plan: Follow your trading plan consistently, regardless of short-term market fluctuations or emotional impulses. Avoid making impulsive decisions based on fear or greed and trust in the effectiveness of your strategy.

Practice Risk Management: Implement effective risk management techniques, including setting appropriate stop-loss levels and position sizing. Managing risk reduces the emotional impact of losses and protects your trading capital.

Continuous Learning and Improvement: Never stop learning and improving your trading skills. Stay updated on market trends, refine your strategy, and seek insights from experienced traders. Continuous learning helps you adapt to changing market conditions and enhances your confidence and decision-making abilities.

Psychology and discipline play a vital role in futures trading. By understanding and managing emotions, practicing discipline, and adopting techniques for developing a strong trading mindset, you can enhance your decision-making process and improve your trading performance.

Successful trading is not just about technical analysis and strategy; it also involves mastering your psychological state.

In the next chapter, we will explore the real-world factors every futures trader must understand, from choosing the right trading platforms and monitoring performance to navigating tax obligations.

PART 10: PRACTICAL CONSIDERATIONS

37: MARKET ACCESS AND TRADING PLATFORMS

In order to participate in futures trading effectively, you need to have proper market access and utilize reliable trading platforms. This chapter will guide you through the process of gaining market access and selecting the right trading platform for your needs.

MARKET ACCESS

Before you can start trading futures, you need to have access to the relevant markets. This involves:

Selecting a Futures Broker: Choose a reputable futures broker that provides access to the markets you wish to trade. Consider factors such as commission rates, platform features, customer support, and the broker's regulatory compliance. Conduct thorough research and compare different brokers to find the one that best suits your trading requirements.

Opening a Trading Account: Once you have selected a broker, you will need to open a trading account. This typically involves providing identification documents, completing the necessary forms, and depositing funds into your account. Follow the instructions provided by your broker to successfully open your trading account.

Market Data and Connectivity: To effectively trade futures, you need access to real-time market data and connectivity to the exchange. Your broker will provide you with access to market data feeds, either for free or for a fee, depending on the level of data you require. Ensure that you have a reliable and fast internet connection to receive up-to-date market information.

TRADING PLATFORMS

A trading platform is the software interface through which you execute trades, monitor market activity, and manage your positions. It is essential to choose a trading platform that is user-friendly, reliable, and equipped with the necessary features for your trading style. Consider the following factors when selecting a trading platform:

Platform Functionality: Evaluate the platform's functionality and features. Ensure it offers real-time market data, order placement, charting tools, technical indicators, risk management tools, and other features that align with your trading strategy and preferences. Test the platform's usability and interface to ensure it is intuitive and meets your needs.

Compatibility and Accessibility: Check the platform's compatibility with your operating system (Windows, Mac, or mobile devices) to ensure seamless access. Consider whether the platform is available as a desktop application, web-based platform, or mobile app, allowing you to trade conveniently from various devices.

Order Execution and Trade Management: Evaluate the platform's order execution speed and reliability. It should provide quick and accurate order placement, modification, and cancellation functionalities. Additionally, ensure the platform allows you to monitor and manage your positions effectively, including setting stop-loss and take-profit levels.

Risk Management Tools: A robust trading platform should offer risk management tools such as position sizing calculators, risk/

reward analysis, and real-time margin requirements. These tools help you assess and manage risk effectively, protecting your capital and optimizing your trading decisions.

Technical Analysis and Charting Tools: Consider the platform's charting capabilities, technical indicators, and drawing tools. A comprehensive charting package enables you to perform technical analysis and make informed trading decisions.

Ensure the platform offers customization options, different timeframes, and the ability to save and analyze historical data.

Backtesting and Strategy Development: If you plan to develop and test trading strategies, check if the platform supports backtesting functionality. This feature allows you to test your strategies using historical data to assess their performance. Additionally, some platforms offer tools for developing and implementing automated trading strategies, known as algorithmic or algo trading.

DEMO ACCOUNTS

Before committing real funds, consider utilizing demo accounts provided by brokers or trading platforms. Demo accounts simulate real trading conditions using virtual funds, allowing you to practice trading strategies, familiarize yourself with the platform, and gain confidence without risking actual money.

Market access and choosing the right trading platform are crucial aspects of futures trading. Select a reputable futures broker, open a trading account, and ensure you have reliable market data and connectivity. When choosing a trading platform, consider its functionality, compatibility, order execution capabilities, risk management tools, technical analysis features, and support for strategy development. Utilize demo accounts to practice and become comfortable with the platform before trading with real funds.

By having the right market access and utilizing a reliable trading platform, you set yourself up for success in futures trading.

In the next chapter, we'll explore how to manage the financial implications of your trading, ensuring that your gains are maximized not only in the market but also after taxes.

38: MONITORING TRADES AND PERFORMANCE ANALYSIS

Once you have executed your trades in the futures market, it is essential to monitor their progress and analyze your trading performance. This chapter will guide you through the process of effectively monitoring your trades and conducting performance analysis to identify strengths, weaknesses, and areas for improvement.

TRADE MONITORING

Trade monitoring involves actively tracking and managing your open positions. Here are some key aspects to consider:

Position Management: Regularly review your open positions to assess their performance and adjust your strategy if necessary. Monitor market conditions, news events, and technical indicators that may impact your trades. Consider setting stop-loss and take-profit levels to manage risk and lock in profits.

Trade Journaling: Maintain a trade journal to record details of each trade, including entry and exit points, position sizes, reasons for entering the trade, and any relevant market observations. This journal will serve as a valuable resource for analyzing your trading performance and making data-driven decisions.

Tracking Market Data: Continuously monitor real-time market data, including price movements, volume, and relevant news. Stay informed about market trends, economic indicators, and events that may impact your trades. Utilize charting tools and technical indicators to analyze price patterns and identify potential opportunities or risks.

Risk Management: Regularly evaluate and manage risk associated with your trades. Monitor your position sizes, margin requirements, and overall portfolio risk. Adjust your risk parameters if needed to ensure you stay within your risk tolerance levels and protect your trading capital.

PERFORMANCE ANALYSIS

Analyzing your trading performance helps you identify strengths, weaknesses, and areas for improvement. Here are key aspects to consider when conducting performance analysis:

Profit and Loss Analysis: Evaluate your overall profitability by analyzing your profit and loss (P&L) statements. Assess the performance of individual trades, including the average profit or loss, win/loss ratio, and risk-to-reward ratios. Identify patterns and trends in your trading results to determine areas where you excel or need improvement.

Risk-adjusted Returns: Consider risk-adjusted returns to assess the efficiency of your trading strategy. Calculate metrics such as the Sharpe ratio or the Sortino ratio, which measure your returns relative to the risk taken. This analysis helps determine if your strategy is providing adequate returns for the level of risk you are exposed to.

Trade Analysis: Dig deeper into individual trades to identify patterns and behaviors. Analyze the entry and exit points, the effectiveness of your trade management, and the impact of market conditions on your decision-making. Determine if there are specific trading setups or strategies that consistently perform better or worse.

Emotional Analysis: Reflect on the emotional aspect of your trading performance. Identify instances where emotions such as fear, greed, or impatience influenced your decision-making. Understanding your emotional triggers and biases can help you develop strategies to manage them effectively.

Trade Execution Analysis: Assess your trade execution to determine if you are effectively entering and exiting positions. Analyze factors such as slippage (the difference between the expected and actual execution price), order fill rates, and execution speed. Identify any issues and make adjustments to improve your trade execution.

LEARNINGS AND ADJUSTMENTS

Based on the insights gained from trade monitoring and performance analysis, make necessary adjustments to enhance your trading approach. This may involve refining your strategy, improving risk management techniques, adjusting position sizes, or addressing emotional biases. Continuously learn from your trades and iterate on your trading plan to adapt to changing market conditions.

Monitoring your trades and conducting performance analysis are essential components of successful futures trading. Actively monitor your open positions, maintain a trade journal, track market data, and manage risk effectively.

Analyze your trading performance by assessing profitability, risk-adjusted returns, individual trades, emotional influences, and trade execution. Use these insights to make informed adjustments and refine your trading approach. By continuously monitoring and analyzing your trades, you can improve your trading skills, optimize your performance, and achieve your trading goals.

In the next chapter, we'll discuss how taxes impact your trading profits, the rules and regulations you need to be aware of, and strategies to optimize your tax obligations.

39: TAX CONSIDERATIONS FOR FUTURES TRADERS

When engaging in futures trading, it is crucial to understand the tax implications associated with your trading activities. This chapter will provide an overview of the key tax considerations for futures traders to help you navigate the tax landscape and ensure compliance with relevant regulations.

TAX CLASSIFICATION

The tax treatment of futures trading can vary depending on your jurisdiction and personal circumstances. In many countries, including the United States, futures trading falls under the category of capital gains or losses for tax purposes.

However, it is essential to consult with a qualified tax professional or accountant familiar with the tax laws in your specific jurisdiction to understand the exact classification and applicable tax rules.

CAPITAL GAINS AND LOSSES

In most cases, profits or gains from futures trading are considered capital gains. Similarly, losses incurred from futures trading are treated as capital losses. The tax rate applied to capital gains can vary depending on the holding period of the futures contracts and your overall taxable income.

TAX REPORTING AND FILING

To comply with tax regulations, futures traders are typically required to report their trading activity on their annual tax returns. This includes providing details of all trades, gains, losses, and any other required information.

Depending on your jurisdiction, specific forms or schedules may be required to report futures trading activity. Ensure that you maintain accurate and detailed records of your trades throughout the tax year.

WASH SALE RULES

In certain jurisdictions, such as the United States, wash sale rules may apply to futures trading. A wash sale occurs when you sell a security (including futures contracts) at a loss and repurchase the same or substantially identical security within a specified period.

Wash sale rules are designed to prevent the immediate recognition of tax losses by disallowing the deduction of losses from wash sales. It is important to be aware of these rules and their implications for tax reporting.

SECTION 1256 CONTRACTS

In the United States, futures contracts are categorized as Section 1256 contracts for tax purposes. This classification provides certain advantages and special tax treatment. Section 1256 contracts are subject to a blended tax rate known as the 60/40 tax rate, where 60% of gains or losses are treated as long-term capital gains or losses, and 40% are treated as short-term capital gains or losses. This tax treatment can have implications for tax planning and reporting.

RETIREMENT ACCOUNTS AND TAX-ADVANTAGED TRADING

If you trade futures within a retirement account, such as an Individual Retirement Account (IRA) or a Self-Directed Solo 401(k), there may be additional tax considerations. Contributions to retirement accounts may provide tax advantages, but distributions and withdrawals may be subject to specific tax rules and penalties. Consult with a tax professional to understand the tax implications of trading futures within retirement accounts.

TAX PLANNING AND PROFESSIONAL ADVICE

Navigating the tax landscape as a futures trader can be complex, and the tax regulations can vary significantly across jurisdictions. It is highly recommended to seek professional advice from a tax professional or accountant with expertise in futures trading and tax law. They can provide guidance on tax planning, ensure compliance with tax regulations, and help optimize your tax situation.

Understanding the tax considerations for futures traders is essential for compliance and optimizing your overall tax situation.

Be aware of the tax classification of your trading activity, report your trades accurately on your tax returns, and be mindful of specific tax rules such as wash sale rules and the treatment of Section 1256 contracts.

Consider seeking professional advice from a tax professional or accountant familiar with futures trading and tax regulations to ensure compliance and make informed tax planning decisions.

In the final chapter, we will provide you with valuable tools, books, and online resources to enhance your knowledge and skills.

40: RESOURCES FOR FURTHER LEARNING AND IMPROVEMENT

As you continue your journey in futures trading, it is essential to stay informed and continually enhance your skills. The financial markets are dynamic, and ongoing education will help you adapt to new developments, refine your strategies, and make informed decisions.

In this chapter, we will explore a variety of resources that can support your growth as a futures trader, including books, online courses, websites, forums, trading tools, and financial news and data providers.

1. BOOKS

Books are a great way to deepen your understanding of futures trading concepts, strategies, and market analysis. Here are some highly recommended titles:

A Complete Guide to the Futures Market by Jack D. Schwager - This comprehensive guide covers everything from basic concepts to advanced trading strategies, making it a valuable resource for traders at all levels.

Trading in the Zone by Mark Douglas - A classic in trading psychology, this book emphasizes the importance of mindset and discipline, essential traits for successful trading.

The New Trading for a Living by Dr. Alexander Elder - This book combines technical analysis with psychological insights, providing practical strategies for trading futures effectively.

Market Wizards series by Jack D. Schwager - These interviews with successful traders offer invaluable insights into their strategies, thought processes, and approaches to the markets.

2. ONLINE COURSES

Online courses are an excellent way to gain structured knowledge and practical skills in futures trading. Here are a few platforms that offer high-quality courses:

Coursera - Offers courses on trading, financial markets, and investment strategies from top universities and institutions.

Udemy - Features a variety of futures trading courses that cater to different experience levels, often at affordable prices.

Investopedia Academy - Provides comprehensive courses covering trading basics, technical analysis, and advanced trading strategies.

TradingAcademy.com - Offers professional trading education focusing on various asset classes, including futures.

3. WEBSITES AND BLOGS

Staying updated with market news and expert opinions is vital for any trader. Here are some reliable websites and blogs:

CME Group - The official website of the Chicago Mercantile Exchange provides market data, educational resources, and updates on futures contracts.

Investopedia - A valuable resource for definitions, tutorials, and articles on trading concepts, strategies, and market news.

Seeking Alpha - A platform for investment research and analysis, featuring articles and insights from experienced traders and investors.

Futures Magazine - An online publication dedicated to futures trading, offering articles, news, and educational resources.

4. TRADING FORUMS AND COMMUNITIES

Engaging with other traders can provide support, insights, and valuable information. Here are some popular trading forums and communities:

Elite Trader - A forum where traders can discuss strategies, share experiences, and seek advice on futures and other markets.

Trade2Win - A vibrant community of traders sharing knowledge and discussing various trading topics, including futures.

Reddit (r/Daytrading) and **r/Futures** - Subreddits where traders can ask questions, share experiences, and discuss strategies.

5. FINANCIAL NEWS AND DATA PROVIDERS

Staying updated with financial news and data is crucial for making informed trading decisions. Here are some key providers:

Yahoo Finance - Offers comprehensive financial news, data, and analysis on various markets, including futures.

CNBC - Provides up-to-the-minute market news and insights, focusing on financial markets and investment strategies.

MarketWatch - Features market news, analysis, and data, including information relevant to futures trading.

Trading Economics - Offers economic indicators, forecasts, and news that can affect futures markets.

The world of futures trading is vast and ever-evolving, and continuous learning is key to your success as a trader. By utilizing the resources outlined in this chapter, you can enhance your understanding, refine your strategies, and stay informed about market developments.

***

Congratulations on reaching the end of *Futures Trading 101: A Step-by-Step Guide and Strategies for Beginner Traders*. Your commitment to learning about futures trading is commendable, and you should feel proud of the knowledge and skills you have acquired throughout this journey.

The road to becoming a successful trader is paved with continuous education and experience. As you apply what you've learned, stay curious, stay disciplined, and embrace the challenges that come your way.

May this book serve as a valuable reference as you embark on your trading journey, and may your future in the markets be prosperous and fulfilling.

ABOUT THE AUTHOR

Usiere Uko

Usiere Uko is a writer, speaker and business and finance coach. Aside from running other businesses, he is involved in helping entrepreneurs grow their businesses and attain their potential through a faith-based business academy and empowerment programs.

Originally trained as a mechanical engineer with extensive experience in the oil industry spanning design, construction, project management and organisational capability, his passion has been to educate people to achieve their fullest potential and live fully through acquiring skills (especially financial skills) to enable them to achieve freedom in other areas of their lives as an integrated whole.

Among the publications he has written for includes Punch (AM Business) and Daily Trust (SME Business) Newspapers, Leadership & Lifestyle and Today's Lifeline magazines.

Usiere lives is happily married with a lovely son and daughter.

BOOKS IN THIS SERIES
ONLINE TRADING FOR BEGINNERS

Day Trading 101: A Complete Beginner's Guide To Trading The Markets

Online Stock Trading 101: A Beginner's Guide To Profitable Trading

Forex Trading 101: A Beginner's Guide And Strategies To Profitable Currency Trading

Scalping Strategies 101: Proven Profitable Trading Tactics For Beginner Traders

Futures Trading 101: A Step-By-Step Guide And Strategies For Beginner Traders

Binary Options Trading 101: A Beginner's Guide To Smart And Profitable Trades

Crypto Trading 101: A Beginner's Guide To

Profiting From Cryptocurrency

Cfd Trading 101: A Beginner's Handbook For Profitable Contracts For Difference Trading

Algorithmic Trading 101: A Practical Introduction To Automated Market Trading For Non-Programmers

BOOKS BY THIS AUTHOR

Practical Steps To Financial Freedom And Independence: Money Management Skills For Beginners

A Simple Guide To Investing In The Money Market: How To Start Making Your Money Work Hard For You

Before You Trade Forex: Things You Need To Know If You Desire To Start Trading Forex Profitably

Before You Invest In Cryptocurrency: A Simple Guide To Understanding The Cryptocurrency Market

101 Common Money Mistakes To Avoid: And How To Fix Them. Book 1: Expenses. Money Management, Making Your Budget Work

How To Invest In Bonds: A Beginner's Guide To

Bonds Investment

How To Invest In Treasury Bills: A Beginner's Guide To Treasury Bonds Investing

How To Avoid Living Under Financial Pressure: A Simple Guide To Getting Back Control Of Your Finances

Financial Independence For Employees: Making Your Job A Stepping Stone To Exiting The Rat Race And Living Your Dreams

Managing Your Money Post Covid: Financial Management Skills For An Era Of High Inflation And Market Disruption

Retire On Your Own Terms: A Simple Guide To Financially Literate Retirement Planning

Your Ultimate Money Makeover: Manage Your Money Better, Take Control Of Your Finances And Your Life

Teaching Kids Money 101: Simple Parenting Strategies For Raising Financially Literate Kids

From Toddler To Teen Years And Beyond

Uncle Ben's Money Lessons: Book I: Do You Want To Work For Money? A Vacation Story With An Adventure Into The World Of Money

Nft Investing 101: A Beginner's Guide To Collectible Digital Assets

Stock Market Investing 101: A Practical Beginners Guide To Online And Offline Stock Trading

Investing In Etfs 101: A Beginner's Guide For Building Wealth With Exchange-Traded Funds

Mutual Funds Investing 101: A Beginner's Guide To Building Wealth Through Smart Investing

Day Trading 101: A Complete Beginner's Guide To Trading The Markets

Options Trading 101: A Beginner's Guide To Trading Stock Options

www.ingramcontent.com/pod-product-compliance
Lightning Source LLC
Chambersburg PA
CBHW060831220526
45466CB00003B/1063